Mary in the Gospel

Translated by
SISTER MARIA CONSTANCE, S.C.H.

MARY

in the

GOSPEL

by Jean Galot, S.J.

The Newman Press
WESTMINSTER, MARYLAND
1965

This is a translation of *Marie dans L'Évangile* by Jean Galot, S.J., first published by Desclée de Brouwer, Paris-Louvain, in 1958.

Nihil Obstat:
REV. DONALD A. PANELLA, M.A., S.T.L., S.S.L.
Censor Librorum

Imprimatur:
FRANCIS CARDINAL SPELLMAN
Archbishop of New York

December 3, 1964

Contents

[v]

Introduction

The purpose of these pages is to sketch out from a few passages of the Gospel which concern Mary a primary Marian theology. We will analyze these passages, one after the other, in an effort to determine their meaning and theological value.

Our study goes beyond the strict domain of exegesis if by exegesis we understand the effort to determine the exact literal meaning of the texts. Other studies which have recently appeared have assumed the task of scrutinizing this literal meaning to draw forth theological theories.[1] While profiting from these works, which however seem to us to have sometimes stretched the simple literal meaning, we will try to take into consideration both what is the immediate meaning of the text, as it was understood and intended by the Evangelist, and the extension which that significance legitimately takes if we compare it with other texts or if we take account of the greater light which the whole of Revelation gives us. It is a legitimate extension because this interpretation which goes beyond the immediate meaning picks up a more profound meaning, which the divine author of Scripture has enclosed in it; the intention of the Holy Spirit in fact went beyond that of the human author and inspired the wording so as to express the truth in accord with the other sacred texts and with the whole message.

It is not a question of making use of accommodative meanings which neglect the original tenor of the text and give it an orientation altogether different from the one it has, as is the case, for example, in applying to Mary texts on divine Wisdom; nor is it a question of freely forging allegorical interpretations. To follow the authentic meaning of Scripture, we must base our interpretation on objective and really characteristic proofs from the text itself. There are suggestions or orientations in the text which the literal meaning leaves still veiled or uncertain, and which can be made strong and clear only by comparisons or theological reflection. We are, therefore, merely developing what remained implicit.

Our first task, consequently, is to establish clearly the literal meaning. Where this meaning is difficult to determine, as in the question addressed by Mary to the angel Gabriel or in the dialog of Cana, we shall proceed by a long, detailed discussion. Then we shall carefully bring to light the theological meaning hidden in the text by pointing out in the interpretation what extends the literal meaning and develops clues to it.

In the brevity of the gospel passages concerning the person and mission of the Virgin Mary, many riches are buried. May we be successful in shedding light upon some of them.

I

※ ※

The Mystery of the Annunciation

I. The Embassy of the Angel Gabriel

The mission of the Angel Gabriel to Mary parallels his appearance to Zachary, in a way that offers striking similarity and contrast. The parallelism between these two announcements certainly did not escape Saint Luke, for it is expressly emphasized in his narrative. Nor had it escaped the source from whom the Evangelist took his account because the whole structure of the narratives, with their specifically Jewish form, is set up according to this parallelism: that source or an intermediate author definitely intended to show the relationship. Our purpose here is not to analyze all the marks of Semitic style that point to an account previous to the one found in Saint Luke, written by a Jew and absorbed by the Evangelist in his Gospel.[1] We merely point out the desire of the Evangelist, as well as of the Jewish source which he used, to make a parallel presentation of the two episodes. This intentional parallelism does not imply any lack of historical fidelity; it simply means that the author of the original narrative recognized several points of contact, striking resemblances, between the two events as they had been related to him, and that he brought them out in his

[1]

narrative by highlighting these component parts and giving them special emphasis.

Furthermore, the author legitimately tried to make his account more reliable by arranging it according to this parallelism, because he recognized therein a divine intention which must be made evident. Like the Evangelist himself, he refrained from introducing any subjective evaluation or interpretation, because he confined himself to relating facts.[2] Nevertheless, the resemblance and the contrast contained in the parallelism suggest certain orientations for theological reflection.

THE TWO MISSIONS

It seems significant that the same Angel, Gabriel, delivered the two messages; this first bond between the two scenes is strengthened by the fact that the Annunciation to Mary took place in "the sixth month" after the conception of John. They are, therefore, two stages of the same undertaking directed by the intervention of an identical messenger.

The difference between the two occasions stands out very distinctly. The Angel Gabriel is sent to Mary; the fact that he was sent is all the more significant because he had appeared to Zachary where angels might more normally be expected: the sanctuary of the Temple, near the spot where the divine presence itself was venerated. The dialog with Mary, on the contrary, was held far from the Holy Place so that the Angel's coming to her seems like a mission to a far country. The Evangelist had not spoken of God's sending the Angel Gabriel to Zachary; the angel's name was given at the moment he appeared to Zachary; but, in Mary's case, we are present, so to speak, at the departure of the angel on his mission.

There is even a reversal of place: Zachary "enters the Temple of the Lord" and finds the angel there; Mary does not move out of her house, for it is the angel who "comes to her" (Luke 1:9, 28). Such a distinct reversal must have some significance. If we consider it in the light of the mystery of the Incarnation, which is about to be accomplished, we seem to see the progress of this mystery traced out for us: God is coming to men to dwell among them. Up to now, men had to go up to the Temple, as Zachary had done, to find the divine presence and to venerate the Lord there; henceforth, God is coming down into the midst of mankind.

In the Old Testament, of course, this current of the Incarnation had been prefigured and anticipated. The book of Genesis relates the visit of God to Abraham (Gen. 18), and the Book of Judges (13) tells of the visit of the angel of God or of God himself to Manue and his wife. In a general way, we may say that, through Revelation, God had entered into the history of man by intervening specially in the destiny of the Jewish people. Sending the Angel Gabriel to Mary is not, therefore, an entirely new mission: God had already come among men. The contrast however, with the appearance of the angel to Zachary implies that his mission indicates a change from the Old Testament: God intends to come to men as He had never come before. Formerly, it was in the Temple that the Lord became, in a certain way, present to his people; the whole Jewish religion held this Temple as center, and the Jews longed for the day when all nations would come there to adore God. Now, in coming to Nazareth, the angel is going to change this center, for God wills to come to the world away from a place of worship. He wants rather to dwell in the midst of mankind.

[3]

The contrast between Zachary's entrance into the sanctuary and the angel's visit to Mary suggests, therefore, the meaning of the Incarnation: God wishes to go outside the presence of the Temple to dwell amongst men. This dwelling is brought to fruition in Mary.

SOLEMNITY AND SIMPLICITY

There is a very sharp contrast in the circumstances of the two messages. The announcement of the Precursor is wrapped in all the solemnity of Jewish worship. It is addressed to a priest in the act of publicly exercising his priestly function. Zachary had been chosen by lot to offer incense on the altar of perfumes; he considered this act, that fundamentally belonged to the power of the highpriest, and could be performed only once in his life,[3] as the crowning glory of his priestly mission, an exceptional privilege of the Lord. It was probably on a Sabbath day for the large gathering of the people mentioned is more reasonably explained in this way.[4] The angel appeared in the holy city, in the Temple, the house of the Lord, more precisely in the sanctuary, close to the Holy of Holies, "at the hour of incense," the time when the people are silently united in prayer with the action of the priest. All the elements, therefore, combine to make it a most solemn occasion; it is at the most solemn point of Jewish liturgy that the angel appears to Zachary.

In contrast with this formality stands *the baffling simplicity of the annunciation made to Mary*. It is not now a priest whom the angel addresses, but a young maiden. All that we are told of her is summed up in one word: her

name is Mary. The Evangelist had noted that Zachary was
of the priestly class of Abia, and added that Elizabeth was
descended from Aaron; she was, therefore, the daughter of a
priest and the wife of a priest. Again we have the contrast:
Mary's origin is not revealed to us. This contrast is more
striking because the origin of Joseph, her betrothed, is not
passed over in silence: he is "of the house of David." Some
exegetes want to refer this to the identity of Mary herself,
applying to her the words: "of the house of David."[5] The
text scarcely warrants this interpretation: it is clearly Joseph
who is meant. But this effort of certain exegetes has at least
the merit of pointing out something strange and contrary to
our natural desires: the omission of all accurate knowledge
of Mary's origin. We would like to find one — the most
honorable — and we regret the silence of the Evangelist in
this regard. Furthermore, the narrative refrains from giving
any praise to the virtues of Mary although praise has been
duly bestowed on Zachary and Elizabeth: "Both were just
before God, walking blamelessly in all the commandments
and ordinances of the Lord" (Luke 1:6). As the standard
praise given to the just men of the Old Testament, it im-
presses the reader with the idea that this husband and wife
deserved to receive a divine favor because of their devout
life. But of the virtue and the antecedents of the virgin of
Nazareth, Saint Luke says not a word, and the source which
he used must have been silent on this point. Doubtless, this
is an indication that the account came originally from Mary
herself who would be very modest and humble in her
manner of relating what concerned herself. Anyway, the fact
remains that it was according to the divine intention that
this inspired text should hold no indication of any remark-

able origin or moral qualification in Mary's lineage. The angel comes to a virgin who apparently offers nothing unusual to single her out and who does not possess the slightest claim to the favor that is accorded her.

Instead of the holy city of Jerusalem, here is a straggling village that had never been named in the Old Testament and, therefore, had no claim to become the theater of a great religious event. Evidently the little village was despised by its neighbors because Nathaniel was to say: "Can anything good come out of Nazareth?" (John 1:46). And it was situated in Galilee, a district which was less genuinely Jewish; so many outsiders lived there that it was called a "district of nations" or "Galilee filled with strangers" (Isa. 8:23; I Macc. 5:15).

There are other circumstances of a like nature. The gorgeous setting of the Temple has given place to an ordinary house like any other house in the villages of Palestine. The exact moment of the arrival of the angel is not mentioned; we know that it is during the sixth month after the conception of the Precursor, but we have no suspicion of the day nor the time of day. Zachary received the message when he was fulfilling the most solemn of priestly functions; but nothing is said of what Mary was doing. There is evidently no sign of any gathering of people; when the crowd watched for Zachary and then saw him reappear unable to speak, they knew "that he had seen a vision in the temple" (Luke 1:22); yet no one could suspect that anything extraordinary had taken place in the little house of Nazareth.

What is the reason for this ordinary setting, the simplest possible? First we should recognize a fundamental characteristic of divine action: *gratuity*. In the announcement of the conception of John the Baptist, God conformed, in a way, to the norms established in the Old Testament; the Incarnation, however, is announced without any semblance of the splendor of Jewish cult. It is a new favor, so gratuitous that no ancient title could claim it. Nazareth is chosen for no other reason than a divine choice itself; Mary is presented to us without any title in order that we may understand that what happened to her is the exclusive work of God. This gratuity also appears in the manner in which the angel makes known his message. He tells Zachary that his petition has been heard (Luke 1:13) to show the part played by his prayer in the favor which has been granted him; to Mary he speaks only of the favor and of divine grace bestowed on her.

Another characteristic of God's design that appears in the arrangement of the various circumstances of the Annunciation may be call the *law of interiority*. The whole exterior setting, however majestic and sacred it might be, is relinquished so that our attention may be directed to the interior realities. Even the beauty and the grandeur of religion in its official ceremonies are effaced, so that only whatever goes on within the soul is of account. No title of noble descent or lineage is granted to Mary so that we may understand that all her worth is within herself. Even more, it seems as if the meeting of the angel is of a more interior nature: Zachary had a vision which filled him with fright, whereas Mary hears a voice which salutes her. There is no spectacle for the eyes, but simply a voice which joins in dialog with her more intimately and with greater recollection.

Finally, the setting of the Annunciation seems to open the way to the universality of the plan of salvation. Do we not detect an intention of universality hidden in that avoidance of a Jewish ritual background, in that mission far from Jerusalem and from the Temple? Is not this same underlying motive in the omission of any reference to Mary's origin, an omission which suggests that no importance must be attached to her race or tribe? Besides, Galilee is a region inhabited by many strangers, consequently, the most likely to imply that the errand of the angel to Mary was of interest not only to the Jewish people, but to all other nations as well. Just as the announcement of the Precursor had taken place in typically Jewish surroundings, the Annunciation of the Saviour tended to break away from this limited horizon. At the moment when Mary is greeted by the angel, she is amid surroundings that suggest an extension of divine action to all mankind.

The setting of the Annunciation, therefore, lends itself to the idea of *gratuity, interiority,* and *universality* which characterize the Incarnation, just as the angel's appearance suggested the coming of God among men. It would be difficult to prove that the Evangelist was aware of the significance of the setting and the angel's mode of procedure.[6] It is in the light of the episode as a whole and from the mystery as we know it, that the details given by the Evangelist take this form; the orientation which they produce results from a theological reflection that the human author of the Gospel had no desire to attempt to express.

II. The Salutation
"REJOICE"

Do we have to see just an ordinary meaning in the first words pronounced by the angel — just a simple "Good day"?

By itself, the Greek word *khaïré* at the opening of a conversation would normally have this meaning, for it was the word commonly used in greeting. Moreover, up to recent times, exegetes agreed in accepting it as a simple greeting. They considered that the term used by Saint Luke was a translation of the Hebrew greeting expressed by the angel in words which wished not joy, but peace ("shalom"). Therefore, *khaïré* could not be taken in the literal sense of "rejoice," but only in the wider meaning of "Good day." It is this wider meaning to which we have become accustomed in the recitation of the Hail Mary since we are used to repeating the words of the angel by saying, "Hail."

Father Lyonnet objected to this interpretation which was natural but not as traditional as might be thought, for it had never been that of the Greek Fathers. They had given *khaïré* the full meaning of "rejoice." Father Lyonnet has shown that this meaning is actually suggested by the text itself.[7] He remarks that in the language of the Septuagint, the term *khaïré*, which is really quite infrequent, never translated a Hebrew greeting but on the contrary held the strong meaning of "rejoice" (Soph. 3:14; Joel 2:21; Zach. 9:9; Lam. 4:21). Since the Gospel of the Infancy, in Saint Luke, borrows its vocabulary from the language of the Septuagint, it is rather this strong meaning that we must use for this word.

As a further indication that it was not a mere "Good day," we can cite the fact that this salutation is missing in the announcement made to Zachary. Now, if it were just a greeting, it should have appeared in both cases; since it was addressed only to Mary, the expression must have a special significance in relation to the message destined for her.

[9]

Secondly, if it were merely an ordinary greeting, it would be accompanied by the name of Mary. Instead, the angel calls Mary, "full of grace" which is by no means customary and suggests something very unusual. Such a way of addressing Mary contains a mystery and is connected with the message; it indicates to us that the *khaïré* is not to be understood in an ordinary, familiar sense.

Furthermore, Mary is troubled and ponders what manner of greeting this might be. The salutation, therefore, seems strange to her and Mary suspects that it holds a deeper meaning, a mystery. The words of the angel sound to her very different from a simple greeting.

Finally, from the point of view of the content of the angel's message, if we do not understand *khaïré* in the strong meaning of *"rejoice,"* there would be no mention of joy although we do find it in the announcement of the Precursor. This would be all the more astonishing because, as Father Lyonnet remarks, the theme of joy is characteristic of the Messianic announcements of the Old Testament: here we have the Messianic announcement par excellence.[8]

All these motives tend to confirm the fact that the term, *khaïré,* must be a faithful translation of the Aramaic expression used by the angel and means, "rejoice." If the angel had saluted Mary with *"shalom,"* Saint Luke would have translated it by the Greek word for "peace" as he does elsewhere in his Gospel (Luke 24:36). Since he reproduced a great number of Semitic expressions in his narrative of the Infancy, he would not have hesitated to preserve the Semitic greeting under the form of a wish for peace. He would certainly have tried to be as literal as possible especially in regard to the words of the angel. We may, then, conclude that the angel really greeted Mary by saying, "Rejoice."

Consequently, it is with an invitation to rejoice that the divine message opens. We can prove that this invitation is of primary importance by stating that the angel who announces to the shepherds the birth of the Saviour will begin with a similar invitation: "Behold I bring you good news of great joy which shall be to all the people . . ." (Luke 2:10). Later, in his teaching, Christ will declare that his goal is to obtain for his disciples a joy that will fill their soul (John 15:11; 16:24; 17:13). Evidently, if the joy of men is the goal sought by Our Saviour, it will hold first place in the words of the angel at the Annunciation, when God reveals his ultimate intention.

To understand better the fullness of the "rejoice" addressed to Mary, we must briefly recall the other times when "rejoice" occurs among the prophets. Let us remember the Messianic announcement made by the prophet Zacharius: "Rejoice greatly, O daughter of Sion, shout for joy, O daughter of Jerusalem: behold thy King will come to thee, the just and savior; he is poor, and riding upon an ass, and upon a colt the foal of an ass" (Zach. 9:9). This is the text applied by the Evangelists to the triumphal entry of Jesus into Jerusalem (Matthew 20:5; John 12:15). The invitation to rejoice is expressly connected with the announcement of the coming of the Messiah-King.

According to the prophets, Sophonias and Joel, the invitation to rejoice was based on the salvation guaranteed by the presence of God in the midst of Israel: "Give praise, O daughter of Sion; shout, O Israel; be glad, and rejoice with all thy heart, O daughter of Jerusalem. The Lord hath taken away thy judgment, he hath turned away thy enemies; the king of Israel the Lord is in the midst of thee, thou shalt fear evil no more. . . . . The Lord thy God in the midst of thee is mighty; he will save" (Soph. 3:14-17). "Fear not, O land, be glad and rejoice, for the Lord hath done great things. . . . . And you, O children of Sion, rejoice, and be joyful in the Lord your God. . . . . And you shall know that I am in the midst of Israel" (Joel 2:21, 23, 27).

In the version of the Septuagint, these three invitations to rejoice use the word *khaïré*. In spite of the absence of this word, at least a fourth text may be added in which the invitation to rejoice is strongly emphasized: the prophecy of Isaias regarding the new Sion. "Give praise, O thou barren, that bearest not: sing forth praise and make a joyful noise, thou that didst not travail with child: for many are the children of the desolate, more than of her that hath a husband, saith the Lord" (Isa. 54:1). Here the invitation to rejoice accompanies the announcement of a marvelous fecundity to her who until then has been barren, a fecundity due to the fact that the Lord wishes to renew spousal relations with Sion.

We feel we are justified in using these previous invitations to throw light on the invitation to rejoice, addressed to Mary. Is not the Annunciation the consummation of the preparations in the Messianic announcements of the Old Testament? The "rejoice" pronounced by the Angel Gabriel would not be understood in its full worth if it is taken separately; it must be considered in the perspective of a whole tradition, as its peak. It sums up in itself what had been promised in the oracles of the prophets.

In the light of these prophetic texts, the ardor of the joy which God wishes to communicate to Mary appears most captivating. "Be glad and rejoice with all thy heart," the prophets had declared in order to mark the violence and plenitude of the Messianic joy. The angel does not ask Mary to leap for joy nor to shout aloud, but he does invite her to a delight which is no less vigorous. We have already observed that there was a law of interiority in the Annunciation. The angel does not exhort Mary to any exterior manifestation of joy; but he does invite her to a joy more intrinsic than that of which the prophets spoke, because it should take possession of her whole being. Within the soul of the Virgin there should be the equivalent of shouts and transports of happiness, a powerful joy which ravishes her whole being.

Comparison with the Messianic announcements of the Old Testament brings up certain other characteristics. In fact, in the Old Testament, the invitation to Messianic joy had been addressed collectively to all the people, to Sion and to her children. Although in the Annunciation the invitation is addressed to Mary individually, this collective meaning could not disappear altogether. Although the angel gives Mary alone the invitation to "rejoice," which formerly had been directed to the nation, it is because in a certain way she personifies the nation. She must rejoice first, but in the name of all, and in order that she may then communicate her joy to all the people. This indicates her mission to the world: Mary is to receive the Messianic joy in the name of mankind, or if you will, in the name of the Church to come, the new Sion.

Furthermore, since in the prophetic oracles, the motive for the invitation to rejoice was the presence of God in the midst of his people, the infallible assurance of their salvation, we must expect that the joy wished for Mary is established on *the presence of God.* The angel will define the manner of this presence more explicitly when he reveals the main point of his message and announces the Incarnation. The "rejoice" of the prophets gives us a presentiment that the presence of God in the midst of Israel will be realized in a special way in Mary, and the rest of the angel's message will point out that it will be under the stupefying form of the presence of the Son of God in the Virgin's womb.

So, this "rejoice" foretells the *coming of the Messiah* according to the words of Zacharias: "Behold thy King will come to thee." This coming of a king is what the angel will explain when he says that the Child will occupy the throne of David.

Finally, the "rejoice" of Isaias, which was called forth by the superior fecundity which God granted to her who had been barren when he takes her for his spouse, orients us toward another aspect of the joy which is to flood Mary's soul: she is "virgin," humanly barren, but she is going to be espoused by God and receive a *marvelous fruitfulness.* In fact, Mary's joy will be greater because the divine action is greater and more miraculous: the virginal motherhood will therefore be a stimulant of happiness.

Evidently, at the moment when Mary heard this "rejoice," she could not grasp the full import of these words and the full meaning that could be attributed to them through comparison with the Messianic announcements of the prophets. But she was to ponder them in her heart, and down through the centuries the Church was to meditate upon them.

This invitation did not necessarily produce in Mary a torrent of joy because it was intended to light up her whole life, not merely a first moment. There is no basis for the claim that it lost its effect because of the trouble aroused in Mary by the angel's salutation. Because of this trouble, Father Jouon rejects the interpretation of *khaïré* by "rejoice." "If Mary had understood it in this way," he maintains, "she would have been immediately flooded with an irresistible feeling of joy, because this invitation coming from God could not fail to take effect. Consequently, Mary would not have been troubled, and the angel would not have had to say to her: 'Fear not, Mary.' "[9] But this is trying to inject into the angel's words a purpose they did not have: there was no question of filling Mary's soul immediately with joy that would have excluded all other sentiments. The "rejoice" needed the full enlightenment of the complete message, and Mary is troubled because this light has not yet been given to her. Accordingly, it was not until the end of the message and at the departure of the angel that joy began to flood Mary's soul. Furthermore, this joy continued to grow quietly in the depth of her heart as the message of the angel penetrated her more deeply through meditation and the added light that subsequent events brought to her.

Father Jouon proposes another objection to the translation, "rejoice." "The Blessed Virgin, it seems to us, did not need an invitation to rejoice; the feeling of joy spontaneously welled up in her heart." It is true that the message of the Annunciation would be enough to excite joy in Mary without any necessity for the actual invitation to "rejoice," but this bidding demonstrates the divine will to spread joy; it is a proof that this joy is a primary objective in the plan of salvation and that it should reign permanently in a soul that has received the announcement of the Messiah.

"FULL OF GRACE"

First of all, let us remark that it is difficult to give an exact translation of the Greek text: there is an alliteration which forms a subtle bond between "rejoice" and "full of grace." By putting the similar sounds of *khaïré* and *kekharitômenè* close together, Saint Luke wanted to make us feel that the call to rejoice had been given to Mary because of her privilege of grace. He may have reproduced in Greek an effect of style which was already found in the Aramaic words pronounced by the angel; according to Father Lyonnet, the Semitic original could be *ronni Muhannah*.[10] If we try to carry over the effect of this alliteration, we could say: "Exult, exalted in grace." The similarity in the words, "exult" and "exalted in grace" suggests that the exultation is closely related to the grace bestowed on Mary.

The word *kekharitômenè* rarely occurs either in Scripture or in profane literature.[11] It could be translated "she who has received grace," but Saint Luke intentionally employed an unusual word. We do not find it elsewhere in his gospel, the Acts of the Apostles, or the New Testament except at the beginning of the Epistle to the Ephesians (1:6). Moreover, Father Lagrange considers that this unusual expression tends to give the idea of an "eminent degree of beauty or of grace."[12]

On the other hand, the words are applied to Mary in

the guise of a proper name and consequently denote a means of recognition. In the sight of the angel and of God whose messenger he is, Mary is characterized by this grace which she possesses. It is not just an ordinary quality which might be shared with others; it is a title which identifies Mary and, is therefore, unique and exceptional.

This is why we are justified in recognizing in this phrase the confirmation of a "singular privilege." How closely does this privilege, considered in the light of the Gospel text, resemble what the Church eighteen centuries later defines under the name of Immaculate Conception? To get the answer we must ask three other questions: What grace is meant? Does Mary possess this grace in its fullness? Does this fullness exist from the first moment of her life?

This grace received by Mary cannot refer to physical beauty; this was the meaning of the word *kekharitômenè* in a passage of Ecclesiasticus (9:8) that counseled not gazing upon a pretty woman. In the context of the Annunciation, it can be interpreted only on the spiritual level as *grace of soul.* If we rely simply on the words of the angel, we cannot draw any conclusion regarding the physical beauty of Mary, her pleasing appearance. It is exclusively a question of divine, supernatural grace.

But since the word could denote appreciation of physical beauty in a woman, it seems that it was used in the angel's greeting in tribute to the *beauty of Mary,* the beauty of her soul. This grace which she had received from God was a special favor that gave singular charm to her soul, an invisible beauty that was radiant and alluring. The angel could appreciate this beauty which was hidden from bodily eyes. In the word *kekharitômenè,* therefore, there is not only an abstract confirmation of the favor with which God has enriched Mary, but an exclamation of admiration from the angel who is enraptured by the charm sent forth by an exceptionally privileged soul.

There remains still greater necessity to determine the exact nature of the divine favor bestowed on Mary. Was it simply an added grace or was it a quality that formed an integral part of Mary's personality? A superficial reading of the text might give the idea that it is enough to consider that the grace granted to Mary was the privilege of having been chosen by God as mother of the Savior. In fact, immediately afterward, the angel declares: "You have found grace before God," and he announces to her that she is to conceive and bring forth a son, the Messiah. Therefore, the grace of which the angel speaks must be related to this motherhood: the divine favor consisted in assigning to Mary that extraordinary mission of motherhood. We might be easily led to conclude that this "grace" was not necessarily a quality intrinsically possessed by Mary; we could satisfy ourselves that Mary has been the object of a divine gift of exceptional benevolence.

The word, *kekharitômenè,* seems to require something more than mere exterior grace. It is certainly true that, according to the explanations of the angel, the grace granted to Mary is essentially destined for the Messianic maternity. But this does not prevent a previous reception of grace by Mary before she becomes the mother of the Savior. Only after the angel sees her and salutes her as full of grace does he make known his message. In order to show the distinction contained in the use of the perfect participle, *kekharitômenè,* which represents a completed action continuing into the present, we would have to translate: "She who has received grace and who continues to possess it." It is not, then, a question simply of the favor which Mary will enjoy when the child is conceived within her, but of a grace already granted which remains permanently within her. Furthermore, this grace belongs to her personally because the word, *kekharitômenè,* is the equivalent of a proper name and because it expresses the beauty emanating from Mary. When Ecclesiasticus uses the word to describe a pretty woman, it leaves no doubt that she really possesses beauty or physical grace. Neither can we doubt that grace has been given to Mary and is her very own.

Is this interior spiritual gift which Mary possesses sanctifying grace? At the time Saint Luke was writing, the notion of sanctifying grace was evidently far from elaboration. But while it still remains vague, the word *kekhatirômenè* inclines us to this meaning because it indicates a divine grace permanently established in a soul. We may infer that this favor has produced profound holiness in Mary since she could be unmistakably identified by this grace: she was therefore thoroughly impregnated with it. But the words of the angel put special emphasis on the gratuity of the divine benevolence which has conferred this grace upon Mary. The angel marvels at the immensity of the sovereign goodness of God, of which Mary is a living witness. She is completely the expression of divine grace.

Next, we must ask ourselves if the word, *kekharitômenè,* permits the idea of a *plenitude of grace* and if the Latin translation, *"plena gratia,"* is justified. There are three indications of a definite notion of plenitude. First of all there is the exact meaning of the verb of which *kekharitômenè* is the participle: this verb, like other verbs of the same model, seems to suggest the idea of overflowing abundance and consequently absolute plenitude.[13] As Saint Luke intentionally made use of this infrequent word, he evidently wanted to give it the full force of its strength, a plenary grace which completely filled the soul of Mary. As further support of this interpretation, we find the word used twice in the Old Testament, in addition to the text of Ecclesiasticus already cited; in both cases it emphasizes a man's moral perfection (Ecclus. 18:17). Father Lagrange translates it, "the perfect man."[14] Judging from these two passages, we would, therefore, seem to be right in thinking that the word, *kekharitômenè,* implies moral perfection and singles Mary out as the perfect woman.

One might show that the mind of Saint Luke could have chosen this consideration to express himself more explicitly, namely the fullness of the Holy Spirit which had been announced by the angel for John the Baptist "even from his mother's womb" (Luke 1:15). If this plenitude was granted to the Precursor in view of his mission, surely a similar plenitude must have been accorded to Mary in view of her maternity.[15] Shortly afterwards, Saint Luke relates that Elizabeth "was filled with the Holy Spirit" (Luke 1:41) when she heard Mary's salutation. If by her presence and her greeting she caused this sudden outpouring of the grace of the Holy Spirit, she herself must have possessed such a fullness. If the word, *kekharitômenè,* expresses a singular and lofty grace, we can scarcely doubt that this grace implies the plenitude that has been granted to others.

We must remember that these suggestions constitute merely an interpretation: we cannot furnish rigorous proof or evidence. It is the interpretation of the Church that gives us an assurance of the exactness of this interpretation and certifies it. Yet it is important to note that this official interpretation agrees with the distinction suggested by the text itself.

The third question is still more difficult: Did the grace granted to Mary exist in plenitude *from the first instant,* from the moment of her conception? This problem never entered the mind of Saint Luke because the question was not raised for many centuries. All that we can say in regard to the term, *kekharitômenè,* is that the perfection or fullness which it suggests was truly complete if it was in her soul from the beginning. Nothing demands this sense of fullness absolutely but it is a logical extension of the strict meaning. Furthermore, the mention that John the Baptist was filled with the Holy Spirit from his mother's womb would demand à fortiori that Mary had been filled with the Holy Spirit from her mother's womb, at the very first moment; there is no absolute proof of this but it agrees thoroughly with the suggestions of the text. Consequently, we may say that the word, *kekharitômenè,* offers a firm basis for the theological acceptance of the privilege of the Immaculate Conception; but this position goes far beyond the conclusions of exegesis.

The first two words of the salutation could be translated according to the connotations we have pointed out: "Rejoice, you who have been steeped in grace." The word, "steeped," represents a fullness that saturates what it fills; it also explains the preoccupation of the angel who is more taken up with marveling at the extraordinary beauty before him than in seeking to make any extension of a privilege.

Mary in the Gospel

"THE LORD IS WITH THEE"

Grammatically, the Greek text could be interpreted either in the form of a wish, "The Lord be with thee!" or by a statement, "The Lord is with thee." The second meaning must have been intended because the divine favor has already been granted to Mary. After the greeting, "You who are full of grace," a wish, "May the Lord be with thee," would be inappropriate because the Lord was already with Mary, since he had granted this grace.

The assertion, "The Lord is with thee," is not superfluous. It refers rather to the future while the expression *kekhari-tômenè* relates to the past. Besides, it concerns especially the mission that Mary will be given to accomplish whereas the words, "full of grace," refer to Mary herself.

We must realize the magnitude of this assurance. It does not point out merely the intimacy which unites Mary to the Lord, a continual presence and companionship with God in the secret of her soul. This assertion is an echo of similar assertions in the Old Testament. To the patriarchs, to Isaac, Jacob, Moses, Josuah, and Gedeon, Yahweh had declared: "I shall be with you" (Gen. 26:3; 31:3; Exod. 3:12; Deut. 31:23; Jos. 1:5; 3:7; Judg. 6:16). Likewise, he had said to David: "I have been with thee wheresoever thou hast walked" (II Judg. 7:9). This declaration is no more than the *formation of an alliance between God and a person who holds in his hand the destiny of the Jewish people*. God strengthens this alliance with the aid which his power furnishes to the person in the mission entrusted to him. The phrase, "I will be with thee," is a solemn promise of assistance.[16]

Thus, the assertion of the angel, "The Lord is with thee," considered in the light of the Old Testament, places Mary among the persons with whom the Lord has formerly made an alliance. This alliance is renewed in her. It applies especially to her but at the same time, like the alliance of old with the patriarchs, with Moses and with David, it encompasses everyone. This is another reason to look upon Mary, at the moment of the Annunciation, as representing Israel and speaking in its name.

The declaration is intended, above all, to assure Mary of *the help of divine power* in the part which she is to play in the work of salvation. Here it is well to recall the conversation between God and Moses. When he learned that he was to deliver Israel from the yoke of Egypt, Moses had said, "Who am I that I should go to Pharaoh and should bring the children of Israel out of Egypt?" God had answered, "I will be with thee" (Exod. 3:11-12). "Who am I?" That question might well come spontaneously to the lips of Mary as she listens to the angel's message. "Who am I to become the mother of the Savior?" The assertion, "The Lord is with thee," forestalls her question.

The comparison with the episode of Gedeon's vocation is also instructive here. When the angel appeared to Gedeon, he began saying, "The Lord is with thee, O most valiant of men." In this way he forestalled the objection of Gedeon who, in being told of his mission to deliver Israel from Madian, protested the lowliness of his family and his own unworthiness; "I beseech thee, my Lord, wherewith shall I deliver Israel?" The Lord repeated the assurance given him at the outset: "I will be with thee; and thou shalt cut off Madian as one man." God promised to supply the warrior with whatever was lacking to him. Now Mary offers this same objection of personal powerlessness insofar as she was unable to become a mother by human means since she wishes to remain a virgin: "How will this be done, since I know not man?" As with Gedeon, "The Lord is with you" has already prepared the answer to Mary's objection of human inability. These words bring to the virgin of Nazareth the assurance at the very outset, that the Lord will supply all her needs.

In addition, greater light will be given her in the message of the Messianic maternity. This message is expressed in the very words used by the prophet Isaias. "Behold," said the angel, "thou shalt conceive in thy womb and shalt bring forth a son, and thou shalt call his name Jesus." "Therefore the Lord himself shall give you a sign," Isaias had said. "Behold a virgin shall conceive and bear a son, and his name shall be called Emmanuel" (Isa. 7:14). Although he bears the name of Jesus, the child who is to be born of Mary is therefore truly the Emmanuel. We know that this name, *Emmanuel,* signifies "God is with us." The Messiah had been foretold as the one who would assure the people of the presence and assistance of God. When the angel greets Mary with the declaration; "The Lord is with you," he is making an allusion to that divine presence promised by the prophet, which he is about to confirm. In the light of prophecy concerning the Emmanuel, the sentence takes on its complete meaning: The Lord is with Mary because it is his will henceforth to be with us. It is through Mary that this definitive presence of God is to be established among us. Here again we see her role as representative and mediatrix of mankind. The mystery, "God is with us," begins to be realized in the truth, "The Lord is with thee." Mary is an integral part of this mystery, an intermediary between God and us.

III. The Notion of Virginity

CONTINUATION OF THE NARRATIVE

The angel's salutation troubles Mary. "When she had heard him she was troubled at his word, and kept pondering what manner of greeting this might be" (Luke 1:29). This trouble resembled that of Zachary; yet it was different. The Greek word used in reference to Mary shows that her trouble is deeper and penetrates her very soul. With Zachary, fright seems to disturb him: "And Zachary, seeing him, was troubled, and fear fell upon him" (Luke 1:12). Whereas Mary ponders over the meaning of the words which have been spoken to her. Unlike Zachary, she remains calm. This is not a vision; these words trouble her and she wonders what they mean. No doubt we could describe this reaction by saying that Mary was suddenly conscious of being confronted by a mystery; that she is momentarily disconcerted, but then she immediately tries to penetrate the meaning. We do not exclude all sense of fear from Mary's concern because the angel will tell her, "Fear not", but this fear merely stimulates her thoughts.

To reassure Mary and to dispel her concern, the angel repeats his salutation in less vigorous terms and in a gentler tone. Instead of the strong exhortation, "Rejoice," he quietly invites her to calm, "Fear not." He no longer uses the official title, "Full of grace," but calls her by her name,

"Mary," and quietly adds, "for thou hast found grace with God."

Nevertheless, we must understand the full import of the words, "Fear not." They are certainly warranted by Mary's concern but, since the whole dialog has an important bearing on the history of our salvation, they must be considered as having a more comprehensive significance. Christ frequently pronounced these words. Although at these times they were prompted by Jesus' desire to soothe the fright of those to whom he addressed them, such as the women in the presence of their Risen Savior, nevertheless they had a much wider purpose, namely, to drive out fear from spiritual attitudes on the new order of salvation. When Jesus told the women prostrate at his feet, "Do not fear," he did not merely want to reassure them and free them from momentary fright, but he expressed the desire that their adoration be not inspired by fear. He desired to form in them an attitude of deep-seated trust because he is bringing salvation to men. In Gabriel's message, which initiates this salvation, the words, "Do not fear," are intended not only to restore calm to Mary's soul but to inspire trust in the Lord fitting to the economy of the New Testament. The angel asks Mary not to show fear but to take the attitude of trustful confidence which must become the fundamental attitude of all Christians in the presence of divine mystery.[17]

After the angel has invited this confidence, he discloses the purpose of his mission and reveals a proposal which is going to cause Mary the greatest emotion. He announces to her that she is to become the mother of the Messiah, of a child to whom "the Lord God will give the throne of

David his father," and "of whose kingdom there shall be no end" (Luke 1:32-33).

Mary does not immediately agree to this proposal. She asks first for an explanation: "How shall this happen, since I do not know man?"

Traditionally, this question of Mary has been interpreted as a proof of her intention to remain a virgin. We are not surprised that certain Protestant exegetes have tried to remove this phrase from the narrative. G. Machen, himself a Protestant, refuting these efforts, has clearly demonstrated that the question asked by Mary forms an integral part of the narrative so that it cannot be separated from the body of the text.[18] But in recent times, an interpretation has appeared among certain Catholic exegetes which refuses to recognize in this sentence an intention of virginity. It is important to explain this point.

INTERPRETATIONS AGAINST THE INTENTION OF VIRGINITY

We can distinguish three interpretations that object to an intention of virginity. The exegesis advanced by Father Landersdorfer[19] finds in the text signs of a misunderstanding between Mary and the angel. According to him Mary believed that the angel was announcing that the conception was already completed; now normally this conception would have implied that the union with Joseph had been consummated. Therefore, Mary countered by declaring to the angel that the marriage had not yet been consummated. The question then would clearly be: "How could this conception of the child take place since one condition is lacking in the fact that I have not yet known man?" These words would indicate that Mary intended to consummate the marriage and that she would have consummated it if the angel had not intervened. Thus the intention of virginity is rejected.

D. Haugg and Father Gaechter follow a different line[20] and try to give a more solid basis to the rejection of any intention of virginity in Mary. They maintain that Mary's having consented to marriage with Joseph is contrary to the hypothesis of a resolution in regard to virginity. "Any one who is bound to God by a vow of virginity does not at the same time become betrothed to an earthly spouse," says Haugg.[21] And Father Gaechter asks,[22] "How could Mary conscientiously give her consent after having made a vow contrary to the real essence of marriage?" We really cannot attribute to Mary knowledge of the subtle distinctions which have been elaborated during many centuries, between the right and the use of the right.

Furthermore, the Jewish milieu by no means encouraged virginity. Haugg especially insists on the fact that in Israel marriage was considered the normal way of life, and virginity not only was not regarded as an ideal but it seemed to be a source of shame, the same as barrenness. Moreover, marriage was sought not simply through natural desire and for the preservation of the nation, but for a much higher spiritual purpose: the desire to have some part in the preparation of the future Messiah. With this thought in mind, every Jewish maiden aspired to a motherhood that might contribute to the coming of the Messiah. Mary had the highest motives for desiring marriage and motherhood.

Before even making any attempt to interpret the text, these authors base their denial of the vow of virginity on two exterior factors: betrothal with Joseph and the Jewish milieu. Father Gaechter, moreover, considers that the passage from Saint Luke is explained better in this way for, if we presume that Mary had made this vow, would not the angel's message have implied God's will to dispense her from it? Or would Mary have preferred her vow, the expression of her own will, to a divine request which seemed to be contrary to it? It would be very improbable; consequently, in the supposition that Mary had made the vow, she would not have set it up as an obstacle to her submission to the divine order; she would not have mentioned it.

What, then, do Mary's words mean? When she heard the message of the angel, she could not have dreamed of a virginal conception because a purely supernatural conception, foreign to all conjugal relation, was an impossibility according to the views of the Old Testament. She thought only of a conception which would take place by natural means. Here was the obstacle: it was still within the period of betrothal to Joseph, before cohabitation with Joseph that would not begin for some months. Though the betrothal to Joseph, according to Jewish custom, would have constituted a definite engagement, it did not permit relations before the betrothed had been taken into the house of the bridegroom. Mary's objection to the angel was therefore her position simply as fianceé, "How shall this happen, since I do not know man?"

According to Haugg and Father Gaechter, this interpretation is the one that follows the text most closely because Mary says, "I do not know man," and not "I shall not know man." The use of the present shows on one hand that she understood the annunciation of the angel, "Thou shalt conceive," as relating to an immediate future and, on the other hand, that she is considering her state of virginity at the present moment without any settled purpose for the future. She states merely that at the present time conjugal relations with Joseph are impossible. But she still intended to consummate the marriage and it is not until after she hears from the angel the miraculous nature of the conception that she will renounce that consummation and resolve to remain a virgin.

J. Auer offers a third interpretation,[23] that Mary's change of mind came before her question. He, likewise, argues that the ideal of virginity was not found in the Old Testament; that it was considered a divine malediction to fail to become a mother; that Mary's betrothal naturally indicated her intention to consummate the marriage. But when the angel makes known to her that she is called to become mother of the Messiah, he simultaneously reveals to her that she is called to give herself completely to God in virginity, since the grace of divine maternity included this vocation. Mary immediately vows virginity but she cannot understand how this virginity can be reconciled with the maternity that has been announced to her. Consequently she asks, "How will this be done, since (according to my real vocation) I do not know man?" The question shows her positive determination to remain a virgin according to the divine vocation, but Mary does not make this decision until after she hears the words of the angel and, therefore, it does not imply any previous resolution of virginity.

Father Audet has offered a solution very similar to this, although he proposed it independently as the result of a more direct exegetical study.[24] He claims that Mary understood that the angel's message was applying to her the prophecy of Isaias (7:14) of a virgin with child, and that she immediately realized that he was proposing a virginal maternity to her. She asks, "How will this be done since (in the hypothesis of the accomplishment of the prophecy of Isaias) I am not to know man?" This exegesis agrees with the preceding one in that it recognizes in the words, "I do not know man," a definite future rejection of marital relations; but it disagrees by accepting only the formation of a hypothesis, without any definite resolution.

EXAMINATION OF THESE INTERPRETATIONS AND
MEANING OF THE TEXT

The denial of Mary's vow of virginity has raised rather spirited reactions and profound discussions to refute the arguments advanced.[25] In fact, some exegetes continue to think with Father Lyonnet, "The most commonly admitted explanation is still the most likely and the most obvious."[26] It indicates a decision of virginity made prior to the Annunciation.

In the first place, Father Landersdorfer's exegesis hardly agrees with the Gospel scene and with the words of the speakers. It implies a misunderstanding between Mary and the angel; it is difficult for us to grant that Mary misunderstood the words of the angel. We would expect a divine messenger to express himself correctly and effectively. Besides, to prove this misunderstanding that Mary believed that the conception had already taken place, we would have to change the tense of the verbs to read, "Thou hast conceived," instead of "Thou shalt conceive," and "I have not

[31]

known man," instead of "I do not know man." Certainly such changes in the Gospel text would be arbitrary.

The third type of interpretation would also involve a change in the tense of the verb in Mary's question. It holds to Mary's rejection of marital relations, but only for the future; it had never occurred to her in the past because the idea came to her through the angel's message. In this supposition, the question would be: "How will this be done since then I shall not know man?" It would require the future rather than the present.

It would also imply that Mary had been informed by the angel of the virginal conception of the child. Although the angel announces to Mary that she is to become the mother of the Messiah, he does not yet reveal the miraculous nature of the conception. There is no allusion to the prophecy of Isaias, nothing to indicate to Mary that it is to be a virginal maternity. Actually, up to the present moment, the angel had repeated that part of the prophecy that announced the conception and birth of the Messiah, and had avoided speaking of virginity. Besides, we can hardly believe that Mary immediately recognized an allusion to this prophecy and drew from it the lessons that an exegete would find in comparing the texts. Therefore, we agree with J. Auer that Mary's vocation to virginity must have been revealed to her at the same time that she received her vocation to motherhood. We could say that Mary had an interior light of grace. But the statement seems unnecessary because the angel made known to Mary what God wished to communicate to her, and we do not see why one part of the message should be transmitted by the angel and the other by interior revelation.

Other interpretations, therefore, seem to have no foundation; the traditional interpretation is much more natural. If we infer from the words, "I know not man," a definite rejection of marital relations, they are explained much better by virtue of a previous decision than by an idea that came to Mary at that moment and brought a sudden change in her dispositions.

The interpretations proposed by Haugg and Father Gaechter have the merit of respecting the sentence, "I know not man," by recognizing a present, and not a past nor a future. However, they do not correspond with that exact shade of meaning that the present tense connotes when used without any further determination. If Mary had wanted to make the objection to the angel that she was not yet cohabiting with Joseph, we would have expected her to ask, "How shall this be done, since I do not yet know Joseph?" Yet the assertion is more sweeping: Mary does not say, "I do not yet know," but more simply, "I do not know." She does not indicate any man in particular as she would have done by saying, "my man" or "the man," namely Joseph; she speaks in a general way and excludes every man. This shows that she is not thinking of the fact that relations with Joseph cannot yet take place and that this is not what she wishes to explain. Her statement has a much wider meaning.

Besides, these interpretations arbitrarily change the meaning of the angel's message and Mary's question. It implies that the angel made it clear that the conception of the child would take place immediately, and that it is this immediate character of the event that forms the obstacle in Mary's eyes. But, in fact, the angel had not spoken of any particular time in the future, "Thou shalt conceive." He had not by any means tried to impress upon Mary that the conception was to take place without delay. No doubt, Mary understood that it would take place in the not too distant future but, since the angel had refrained from stating the exact time, this was not the thought that preoccupied her and made her raise an objection. Since the angel had not said, "At the present moment thou shalt conceive," Mary did not say, "How shall this be done at the present moment, since I do not know man?" She is just as indefinite as the angel in regard to the time. The message was concerned with the fact and not with the time of the maternity; it is also to this fact that Mary's question was directed, concerning "how."

Finally, if Mary's objection had been drawn from her state of mere betrothal, it would have little weight. Any difficulty in that regard would have been easily overcome. On the other hand, if Mary intended to consummate her marriage with Joseph, she would have found that the angel's message came just at the moment to predict the destiny of a child who would be born of that marriage. The day of the marriage could be advanced if necessary. It is true that the period of betrothal was regularly twelve months but rabbinical texts show that this interval could be shortened or even that the marriage could take place immediately after the betrothal.[27] We must remember, too, the nature of betrothal among the Jews. The statement made by Philon, a contemporary of Mary, is particularly interesting; he considers that the betrothals are as binding as marriage and, therefore, that a sin committed with the fiancee of another is adultery.[28] Betrothal was a formal contract; consequently, there would be much less difficulty in hastening the day on which the bridegroom introduced the bride into his home.

Therefore, the difficulty of advancing the marriage date would have been a very petty objection for Mary to raise against such a great message from the angel. It would have meant that, after she had listened to the remarkable greatness of the child who was promised, Mary would have been insisting on a detail that had not occurred to the angel: the arrangement of the date of her marriage. Did such a petty detail warrant the question, "How shall this be done?" Would we not be judging Mary to be very small-minded to let herself be obsessed by a difficulty of secondary importance in the face of the tremendously great prospect described by the angel?

The unequivocal words that frame the question lead us to understand that Mary's reason for objecting is much more serious and much more worthy of consideration.

An examination of the various interpretations opposed to the idea of virginity shows that each one tries to introduce changes in the verb which do not altogether agree with the suggestions of the text: "I have not known man"; "I shall not know man"; "I am not to know man"; "I do not yet know the man." It seems preferable to accept the sentence, "I do not know man," which in plain terms probably expresses just what Mary wants to say.

In this sentence, Mary affirms her virginity absolutely, because she excludes relations with all men, not merely Joseph; "man" used without the article leaves the word undetermined.

Mary makes this affirmation of virginity in the present tense, but the present tense may be used to make a general assertion that applies to any time, future as well as past. We have indications that Mary intended to add strength to her statement in this way. First, as we have noted, she makes no reference to any definite time; she does not set any limits by a "now" or a "not yet," but declares without restriction: "I do not know." She speaks, therefore, as if her virginity was a permanent, unchangeable state. The very fact that she proposes this virginity as a difficulty in regard to the angel's message only serves to corroborate the finality of her decision: there would be no serious difficulty unless she intended to remain a virgin. Mary protests her virginity as an obstacle so great that she can discern no human solution for the problem of her maternity. She puts the question to the angel very distinctly because the difficulty can be resolved only through him, outside of natural means. Therefore this virginity is a state which Mary is resolved to maintain and which in her mind is unchangeable.

Since this difficulty really concerns the future, we might wonder why Mary did not use the future tense, "I shall not know man." The present was the simplest and most effective way for her to express herself. In fact, at that moment of the Annunciation, Mary is suddenly confronted with a future full of mystery, a future in which she will be led by God along extraordinary paths. Therefore, she avoids saying what she will do in the future because she understands that she must not interfere with God's designs and wants to leave herself completely in his hands. Careful not to presume on his intentions in regard to her, she does not say, "I shall remain a virgin," but "I am a virgin." This prudence was all the more requisite because the maternity which had been announced to her did not at first sight accord with her virginity. As Father Lagrange remarks, "There was a reason to keep in the present, namely, not to be too ready to state a resolution which, as soon as the angel has spoken, could appear to be contrary to the designs of God."[29]

Mary's words show a sensitivity toward the divine will which is not yet fully revealed to her. She desires to state simply what is certain, because she knows that she is binding herself to virginity through divine inspiration. Therefore, she affirms that she does not know man, indicating that she intends to continue in virginity; she knows that this intention at least conforms to the will of God. But her statement is forceful, though respectful, and Mary is careful not to set up her own will as the inflexible law to decide the future. She does not want to order her own future, but submits herself to God's designs for her. That is why she takes care to say, "I do not know man," rather than, "I shall not know man."

Consequently, if we analyze Mary's statement, we must recognize it as:

1. A general affirmation of virginity in regard to every man without exception and stated in simple, unequivocal terms, without restriction of time.

2. A strong affirmation, presented as an obstacle to the divine message, serious enough to be given as an objection to the angel only if it concerned a permanent condition of virginity, making motherhood impossible by natural means.

3. A discreet affirmation, perfectly conformable to the will of God, master of the future, and therefore mentioning only a present state of virginity with the understanding of her existing resolution to preserve it.

Mary, therefore, succeeds in expressing her interior dispositions in a few words exactly suited to her present situation. These words are so simple that at first sight they might seem too vague and we might be tempted to complement or correct them; but if we take them literally, according to the full force of their meaning, we find that they contain a firm intention of remaining a virgin.

We might well wonder what the inspired author, Saint Luke, was thinking as he copied down Mary's words. Did he recognize that promise of virginity which subsequent exegesis found in them? In all probability, he must have seen there the expression of an ideal whose strength and beauty had been known from the beginning of Christianity. Had he not been the companion of Saint Paul who had praised with great fervor that ideal of virginity which he practised and who had emphasized that such an ideal permitted a woman to consecrate herself completely to the Lord in mind and in spirit? (I Cor. 7:32-34) It would be surprising if Saint Luke, in writing down the story of the Annunciation, had not discerned in Mary's words the first manifestation of this ideal and had not recognized the mother of Christ as the woman who before all others desired to consecrate her virginity to the Lord and "be holy in body and in spirit."

THE BETROTHAL WITH JOSEPH IN THE JEWISH MILIEU

As we do not know the circumstances of Mary's betrothal to Joseph, we cannot say exactly why she had accepted the prospect of marriage with Joseph while she still intended to remain a virgin. We must suppose that according to custom this marriage had been proposed by her father.[30] It is likely that Mary looked upon her father's arrangement as an indication of God's will. She probably thought that this marriage would be a protection to her virginity so that her duty of obedience to her father corresponded with her aspiration of remaining a virgin. In fact, since profession of virginity was by no means a general practice in Israel, marriage was the only way to assure herself of tranquility and to provide for her future. If Mary had good reason to think that Joseph was willing to respect her virginity, such a marriage was the ideal solution. So she had consented to the marriage considering it a providential opportunity which, far from making her abandon her virginal consecration, allowed her to fulfill it with greater security.

Evidently a marriage accepted under such conditions was an exceptional case. It was just as exceptional as the resolution of virginity itself. Here we run up against the argument that this exceptional decision was practically impossible because the Jewish milieu was unfavorable to the whole idea of virginity.

It is easy for us to conclude that it was very unlikely that Mary resolved to remain a virgin, if we look upon her merely as a young girl subject to the influence of an environment in which the main ambition of all women was marriage and motherhood. But we must picture Mary's life in the context of grace in which she developed. When we take into consideration the grace of the Immaculate Conception and the extraordinary plenitude of holiness which accompanied it, we find it normal that Mary desired to belong entirely to the Lord. It seems inevitable that Mary, enlightened and motivated by this grace, would aspire to

this virginal consecration as so many souls would in the days
to come. The Holy Ghost would certainly have suggested to
her this gift of self that He would propose later to so many
young girls, that was so appropriate to the mission which
would devolve upon her. And how could Mary have failed
to respond to this grace? The fact of the Immaculate Conception, therefore, overthrows the conjectures that would
be drawn from purely human and natural conditions. We
cannot ignore it when we examine the psychology of Mary
before the Annunciation.

In order to follow this inspiration, it was not necessary for
Mary to have before her eyes any formal practice of virginity. She did not need any judicial setting, any formula
or ceremony, to vow her love to God; as with so many
others after her, it was in the secret of her heart that she
took the resolution of remaining a virgin. This resolution,
moreover, must not be given the name of vow if we understand by the vow of virginity a promise made in specially
prescribed form.

On the other hand, we do not have to deny that Mary
may have found in her own Jewish environment a certain
esteem for virginity; the idea of perfect chastity in a spirit
of consecration to God was not unknown, because certain
groups of Essenes practised celibacy, and the Precursor John
the Baptist was to follow the same course. Evidently, this
path was not used exclusively by men because Philon mentions the presence of virgins in the Jewish sect of "the
Therapeutes"; he emphasizes the fact that they observed
chastity not through obligation, but of their own accord,
and that this mode of life was intended to make them ready
for contemplation.[31] This example shows that the ideal of

virginity among women was not completely absent from Judaism and that it was held in esteem by an author like Philon, a contemporary of Mary. Shall we say that this idea, practised by Jewish women, was inconceivable for Mary?

Furthermore, a Qumrân document implies that the ideal of virginity had made progress and was more highly regarded among fervent Jews in the period immediately preceding the coming of Christ.[32] The idea was spreading that the service of God demanded complete chastity. The Jewish milieu could, therefore, lend support to Mary in her desire to consecrate her virginity to the Lord.

Finally, it may be argued that Mary's virginity responds to a special grace of the Christian order because it has meaning only as a consequence of the divine maternity or implication in it; it was not to enter the mind and will of Mary until after the message of the Annunciation. Therefore Mary would have taken this resolution only on becoming the mother of the Lord. Before that time, she still belonged to the economy of the Jewish religion and was not yet ready for her virginal consecration.

The argument does not hold because, if we must admit that Mary's virginity is a consequence of her maternity according to the requirements of the divine plan, we must conclude that the decision of virginity was made after she gave her consent to the maternity or at the same time. It is very true that Mary was called to virginal consecration by reason of her destiny as mother of the Son of God. But, the grace of the Immaculate Conception is likewise implicated in the grace of the divine maternity and is a consequence of it. But the grace of the Immaculate Conception preceded in time the grace given at the Annunciation; and furthermore, this grace belonged to the Christian order since it was granted to Mary in view of her participation in the mysteries of the Incarnation and the Redemption. Must we not then agree that the grace of a vocation to virginity, although enjoined by the divine motherhood, could come before it in time, could inspire Mary long before the Annunciation, and nevertheless be a grace of the Christian order? Not only was this antecedence of time possible; it was most fitting because it was right that Mary should have been for some time consciously preparing herself by her resolution of virginity for the divine maternity of which she was yet unaware. Thus, it was really a Christian virginity that was asked of Mary because Christianity was being made ready in her.

IMPORTANCE OF MARY'S VIRGINAL CONSECRATION IN THE ECONOMY OF SALVATION[33]

In regard to the virginal consecration proved by the declaration, "I do not know man," we must repeat what we have already noted about other details of the narrative of the Annunciation: it is not enough to think of it as a resolution affecting Mary's own personal life. Since there are indications that Mary represented the Jewish people and mankind at that moment, we must consider the universal importance this virginity must assume. Since the angel deliberately formulated his message to arouse Mary's protestation of virginity, Mary's purpose of virginity evidently had a definite part to play in the unfolding of the plan of salvation and especially the divine maternity.

We must consider Mary's consecration to virginity not as a

form of holiness contrary to the ideals of the Old Testament but rather as the acme of the spiritual journey of the Jewish people. We have already noted that the angel had greeted Mary with the phrase, "Rejoice"; this had been traditionally addressed to the chosen people and thus seemed to testify that the privileges granted to Israel were culminating in Mary. Virginal consecration was an integral part of the marvelous grace found in her. How then was this grace, granted to Mary, a culmination of the spirituality of Judaism?

Mary's renunciation of motherhood was an exceptional act, but it proceeded from a fundamental disposition of soul that had been developed and praised insistently in the Old Testament: *poverty in the sight of God*. By waiving all human ambition of a large family and depriving herself of her capacity for motherhood, Mary made herself "poor." She stood before the Lord stripped of a noble wealth other women coveted, future descendants. Never before had poverty been pushed so far, never had it penetrated a woman's heart so deeply that it robbed it of its most cherished desire, motherhood. Mary brought to a peak the disposition of poverty which the Sacred Books had taught her was so precious in the sight of God.

If Mary allied herself to the poor of the Old Testament through her virginity, she was likewise aligned with those women whose barrenness had been specially blessed by God and made fruitful. Sara, the wife of Abraham, Anna, the mother of Samuel, and Elizabeth, the mother of John the Baptist, manifested the divine will to grant to a barren woman a child of great destiny. By human barrenness, God wishes to show that from divine power comes a chosen offspring. The idea that *woman must look to God for her fruit-fulness* seems already to be in the background of the story of the fall in Genesis.[34] This idea gradually grew clearer as it became more certain that salvation was to be brought about not by men but by God. Thus men whom God wished to raise up to come to the aid of mankind would owe their birth to divine intervention, made more striking by a mother's barrenness. If this line of development is to be considered the prophecy of Isaias regarding the virgin who has conceived and who brings forth Emmanuel,[35] the prophecy in which the Messias appears as rising not according to normal human generation or royal dynasty, but through a superhuman and virginal conception, a sign given by God, this line of development has now reached a climax with Mary. It would be inexact, then, to say that Jewish tradition could not have prepared Mary for the practice of virginity. Although it had not been followed, this practice was consonant with important events in the history of Israel. Mary easily could have understood from the Old Testament that human barrenness could be particularly pleasing to God and an instrument of divine action in this world. Without the slightest suspicion of the motherhood to which she was destined, she realized that her virginity would be agreeable to God and that she was to place in His hands all hope of fruitfulness from her life.

Mary, therefore, is *the epitome of what the Old Testament had judged "poor" and of women willed by God to be humanly barren in view of a higher fruitfulness.* Mary summarized in herself the destiny of poverty and of barrenness, but by carrying it to perfection deliberately willed interior poverty and human barrenness. Mary had so well understood the divine Intention at work in these forms of poverty and barrenness that she had chosen this state for herself and had spontaneously elected a situation which had not been a matter of choice to others. Thus, her resolution of virginity carried on, went beyond, and led to the summit of the spirit of the Old Testament.

Mary's proposal of virginity was firmly rooted in Jewish tradition not only under a negative aspect of deprivation and barrenness, but also a positive one of consecration to God. G. Vermes notes that, according to the Qumrân scroll, the "sons of light" were obliged to observe chastity because nearness to God required of men an angelic life. Still more striking was the rabbinical legend that Moses had preserved continency and had ceased to know his wife after God appeared to him in the burning bush.[36] Whoever became intimate with God must relinquish intimacy with man.

If we examine fully the positive notion of virginity, we find that virginity is a love of a higher order, a love that is given directly and personally to God which can be compared with the love of one spouse for another because it is a complete surrender of self.

Mary had found God's desire for this love in the Old Testament. Through the mouth of the prophets, the Lord had announced the ideal love which would one day bind his people to him, that of spouse for spouse. In the Canticle of Canticles, that love had been represented by images replete with vivacity and enticement. As she listened to these passages of Scripture, Mary must have been predisposed to recognize the call which they contained and to try to respond to it. If we consider her interior disposition, how can we help but think that she desired to conform to this picture of Israel with the divine Spouse, and to vow the love of a humble spouse to God?

It is true that at the moment of the Annunciation, she speaks of her resolution to virginity in a negative way, because she wishes to mention a difficulty concerning the motherhood which the angel is proposing to her. But this negative expression: "I know not man," re-echoes a prophecy of Osee in which God says to His people: "And I will espouse thee to me forever: and I will espouse thee to me in justice, and judgment, and in mercy, and in commiserations. And I will espouse thee to me in faith: and thou shalt know that I am the Lord" (Osee 2:19-20). The goal of the divine espousals was that Israel should know God and him alone after so many past infidelities. Mary's sentence, "I know not man," translates exactly *the attitude of a spouse who wishes to know only Yahweh.* We do not claim that when she pronounced it, the Blessed Virgin was thinking of the prophecy of Osee nor for that matter any other passage of Scripture. At that moment she was expressing her personal feeling in the simplest way. But this personal feeling had been formed from familiarity with prophetic oracles like the one we have just cited. When we seek to place Mary in a Jewish milieu, we must first of all take account of the fact that her mind had been completely molded to the spirit of the Old Testament, particularly to that prospect of association with God as close as conjugal love. It is the kind of love that animates Mary's declaration to the angel; above all, it is a love that assures her fidelity, for it is that she may know God alone that Mary wishes to know no man.

Thus the love of a faithful spouse for the Lord, that ideal relationship which had been foretold for Israel, is actualized in Mary at the time of the Annunciation. This realization helps us to understand better how Mary expresses her resolution of virginity in the name of the whole nation because that resolution affirms the tender love of the divine betrothal. The marvelous idyll foretold by the prophets and by the Canticle is realized perfectly in the Blessed Virgin.

Mary stands at the peak of the Old Testament, summing up in her resolution of virginity the concept of poverty basic to her religion and bringing it to fulfillment in her promise of a union of love with the Lord. To complete this idea, let us add that the grace through which virginity had blossomed in Mary was Christian, and in representing the nation, Mary not only holds the place of Israel but more universally she represents the ideal people of the future, the Church open to all mankind.

Therefore, it is *in the name of the Church,* which she unwittingly represents by virtue of the divine plan, that she announces her intention of remaining a virgin in her motherhood. In this utterance she preludes the practice of Christian virginity. That is why Saint Augustine will recognize Mary's "vow of virginity": he will base his assertion not only on the meaning of the words related by Saint Luke but also on the assumption that Mary is the origin, the model of virginal consecration as it is practiced in the Church.[37] Here the gospel text contains a first orientation toward this principle in the indications that the Virgin of the Annunciation holds the place of the ideal Sion; consequently, her virginity is destined to be communicated to the Church.

IV. The Consent to Maternity

THE ACT OF FAITH

A comparison with the announcement of Zachary draws our attention to the act of faith made by Mary. Remarkable among the superior aspects of the second annunciation is the receptivity of the Blessed Virgin in believing the words of the angel. First, we note a difference between Zachary's question and that asked by Mary. Zachary wants to know how he will be able to recognize the truth of the message because his wife and he are advanced in age. Mary, on the contrary, does not seek assurance of the truth of the maternity announced to her, and desires simply to know how it will be accomplished: "How will this be done?" She has no doubt that it will be done, but inquires how it will come about.

Nevertheless, although this comparison of the two questions may be revealing, it can leave the reader rather uncertain as to the interior disposition that animated them: the extent of Zachary's doubt and the firmness of the Blessed Virgin's faith. These uncertainties are dispelled by the information with which the Gospel itself completes the story. The angel gives Zachary a sign which is also a punishment for his incredulity as he frankly tells him: "because thou hast not believed my words, which will be fulfilled in their proper time" (Luke 1:20). The praise which Elizabeth addresses to Mary at the Visitation corresponds with this reproach: "And blessed is she who has believed, because the things promised her by the Lord shall be accomplished" (Luke 1:45). This praise is certainly motivated by Mary's behavior. When Elizabeth heard the salutation of her cousin, she immediately compared it with the silence and the absence of salutation on the part of Zachary; thus she was led, we may suppose, to distinguish in Mary's salutation, the sign of her faith. It is important to emphasize that this praise was offered at the moment when Elizabeth was filled with the Holy Ghost, and guided by divine illumination. It is praise inspired by God that guarantees the excellence of Mary's faith at the time of the Annunciation.

Elizabeth's words also give us an idea of the importance of this faith, since Mary is called blessed because of it: therein lies its merit. Furthermore, the account of the Annunciation implies that the angel's message had been composed to stimulate this virtue. It is a fearless trust that he asks of Mary when he announces the maternity to which God destines her without revealing, at the same time, how it will be brought about. Evidently it would have been possible for God to announce simultaneously the conception of the Messiah and the miraculous operation of the Holy Ghost, and thus to have avoided the difficulty of reconciling motherhood with her consecration of virginity. Instead of making Mary's act of faith easier, the angel has deliberately tried her confidence: he holds out motherhood to her without revealing how her virginity is to be respected and, consequently, he leaves her in ignorance of an essential factor. It is in this ignorance that she is to testify to her faith, "to believe that the things promised her by the Lord shall be accomplished." So, the first response that God asked from Mary was faith, a faith which was all the more meritorious because the message was designedly mysterious.

Mary gives this response. She distinguishes herself by the greatness of her faith precisely because she has been prepared for it by her virginity. In fact, her act of faith coincides with her protestation of virginity, for it arises from the same disposition of soul. The resolution of virginity is based on a trust placed in God alone; by renouncing all hope of human motherhood, Mary had resigned all the fruitfulness of her life into the hands of God. When she renews her resolution in response to the angel's message, she is maintaining that trust and it is that same trust that makes her believe in the maternal fecundity which God promises to her. Therefore, it is the trust intrinsic to her virginal consecration that makes her surmount the obstacle which this virginity constitutes in regard to the maternity offered to her. Mary resigns herself to the divine omnipotence that is able to make her human barrenness fruitful.

This first act of faith implied in the question, "How shall this happen, since I do not know man?" will be confirmed in the definitive act of faith contained in the assent given to the angel's proposal. The text also indicates that the angel requires this act of faith with the consent: he enlightens Mary on the miraculous nature of the conception; then he announces a sign, the child granted to Elizabeth; and he ends with these words: "for nothing shall be impossible with God." These words are an enjoinment on her faith.

It is significant that at this decisive moment in the history of mankind, it is first of all an attitude of faith that is required from Mary. This is the *first form of cooperation* that God asks of the creature in carrying out His plan of salvation. This faith consists *in a trusting readiness to let God work out His designs*. This is the readiness that Mary shows toward the coming of the Messiah.

We must not lose sight of the universal implication in this

act of faith. At the moment of the Annunciation, Mary's faith is the apogee of the faith of Israel; it sums up and perfects a faith gradually developed by Jewish tradition which amounted to a non-reliance on human resources by the people but complete trust in the Lord whom they recognized as the one God and their only Savior. This act of faith, that is to inaugurate the New Testament, recalls and renews Abraham's act of faith which had inaugurated the Old Covenant. According to the account in Genesis, the Lord had demanded this first act of faith by testing Abraham with the paradoxical promise of a numerous posterity that would be born of him when he was old and childless. "Abraham believed God, and it was reputed to him unto justice" (Gen. 15:5). And Abraham, who "hoping against hope, believed" (Rom. 4:18), was revered by the Jews as the origin and the model of Israel. Now at the Annunciation, the divine message follows a similar pattern: it makes a promise to Mary which is seemingly impossible because of her state of virginity. Just as Abraham had believed in the power of God to reconcile a promised posterity with Sara's barrenness, so Mary believes in God's power to reconcile a promised motherhood with her virginity. In both cases, there is truth in the omnipotence of God to surmount absolute human impotence, and this trust merits a marvelous posterity.[38]

Nevertheless, we must note the superiority of Mary's faith: nature imposed an obstacle on Abraham's fatherhood, but with Mary the obstacle to motherhood was not imposed upon her. Yet the Blessed Virgin, still believing that the promise would be fulfilled, asserts her will to maintain it in the face of the angel's proposal. Both an analogy and a superiority are present in this sacrifice. Mary's faith, like that of Abraham, will be put to the test and reach its highest intensity in the sacrifice of her son; her trial will be more painful because she has been warned by the angel that Jesus is the Savior and that consequently she has far greater reason than Abraham to concentrate all her hope in him. When the overwhelming drama of Calvary apparently destroys this hope, Mary's faith will be more heroic than that of Abraham. The striking parallelism between these two attitudes of faith, required by God at two different stages in the Revelation and the Covenant with men, helps to show the importance of faith in the divine plan of salvation.

In that mission of summing up the faith of the Old Testament, Mary not only brought to perfection the faith inaugurated by Abraham; she made up for all the insufficiencies of the faith of Israel and compensated for the unbelief of the Jewish people and their leaders. An incident comes spontaneously to mind in which the prophet Isaias had announced, "Behold a virgin shall conceive and bear a son, and his name shall be called Emmanuel" (Isa. 7:14). Before making this prophecy, Isaias had asked King Achaz to make an act of faith, to renounce his own plans, particularly a projected alliance with Assyria by which he wished to save his people, and to place all his trust in the Lord who assured him that he need not fear his present aggressors. Achaz had not been willing to believe in this assurance and had even refused to ask for the sign that the prophet was offering as a pledge. In reply to this unbelief, Isaias had revealed the sign of the virginal conception of the Messiah. Since the representative of the line of David refused to believe, the Messiah would not be born of that dynasty by way of human generation. He would be the son of a virgin and would be conceived through divine power. In the light of this episode, along the course of Jewish history between Abraham and Mary, we understand better why God first asks an act of faith from Mary. The act of faith that King Achaz would not make before the announcement of the virginal conception of Emmanuel must be made by Mary before this conception may take place. In the eyes of the Lord, the excellence of Mary's faith is to wipe out the deficiencies of the faith of the Jewish nation. In the name of Israel, she is called to make an act of faith to repair the unbelief of the past, as the fidelity of her protestation of virginity repairs the infidelities of the people in their love for the Lord.

By summing up the faith of the past and perfecting it in herself, Mary pledges the faith of the future. Since, in the Annunciation, she represents God's people according to its broader meaning, her act of faith is made in the name of the Church rather than in the name of Israel. Her faith is identical with that of the Church, because it possesses the essential characteristic of bearing directly on Christ. This is distinct from the faith of the Old Testament. Therefore, we may say that *the faith of the Church is born in the soul of Mary.*

THE REVELATION OF THE DIVINE SONSHIP OF JESUS

When we say that Mary's act of faith at the Annunciation already contained the substance of the faith of the Church since it bore directly on Christ, we do not pretend that this first act of faith in the New Testament had the full development that faith would assume once Christ should have fully revealed Himself in his work of redemption. It is only a beginning in embryo of what is to follow. Mary's faith had not been fully enlightened since the form of redemption by the death and resurrection of Christ is passed over in complete silence at the Annunciation.

Did Mary's faith at that time accept the divine sonship of Jesus and did she understand from the words of the angel that she was being asked to consent to a divine maternity? When she gave her consent, did she know that he who was to be her son was God?

Twice the angel calls the child Son of God. But the context in which this title is used to show the meaning does not correspond exactly with the present-day significance. When we speak of Christ as Son of God, we mean that he is the second Person of the Trinity, eternally begotten by the Father and having a divine nature identical with His. The angel does not go so far in his disclosure. He definitely tells Mary that her child "shall be great and shall be called the Son of the Most High." But he immediately makes it clear that this sonship is meant as a designation of the Messiah. In fact, he adds, "and the Lord God will give him the throne of David his father, and he shall be king over the house of Jacob forever; and of his kingdom there shall be no end" (Luke 1:34). The title of "Son of the Most High," as it was explained by the angel and as it was definitely to be understood by Mary, therefore, signified that Jesus would be the Messiah. For the humble young maiden of Nazareth, that in itself was an astounding revelation, even without the disclosure of the divinity of the Incarnate Word.

The second use of the title marks an advance over the

first revelation. In answer to the question asked by the Blessed Virgin, the angel says: "The Holy Spirit shall come upon thee and the power of the Most High shall overshadow thee; and therefore the Holy One to be born shall be called the Son of God" (Luke 1:35). This means that the child will be Son of God in a sense other than the Messianic meaning. He will be Son of the Most High not only through adoption, by virtue of a choice of divine love which raises him to a supreme rank, but through generation, since the power of the Most High will act in Mary to make her a mother. It adds light to the revelation but not full understanding. As Maldonat says, "The angel does not treat of the nature of Christ, but of the manner of his generation."[39] If the divinity of the child was to be clearly affirmed, it would have been necessary to allude to the eternal generation of the Son or to the divine nature which He possessed in his own right; but mention is made only of his temporal generation in the womb of the Virgin.

Mary could understand from these words only that the Most High would be father of her child by reason of this miraculous conception operated through Him. Indeed, this temporal generation was the sign of the eternal generation. There was in fact an essential difference between the miraculous maternity granted to Mary and that by which the wives of the patriarchs and Elizabeth had been blessed. Previously, God had given birth to the child through the co-operation of a human father so that the conception resulted from a union according to the flesh. In Mary's case, on the contrary, this union was set aside, and without the cooperation of a human father God alone operated through his power or his Spirit in the womb of the Virgin. It was God's will, therefore, to affirm his sole paternity of the child. If we wonder why God rejected all human paternity, we seem to find only one reason, namely, his will to show that this child was factually his Son. The virginal conception was intended to reveal the divine sonship of Jesus. Therefore, through meditation and study of the mystery of this conception miraculously operated by God in her virginal womb, Mary could discover the full import of this sonship of Jesus with regard to the Father. But at the moment of the Annunciation, the divinity of Christ was only an implicit truth; Mary could not have recognized it clearly. The mere announcement of the extraordinary intervention of the Holy Ghost was enough to astound her and claim the full measure of her faith.

Was there anything else in the angel's message which might have further enlightened her faith and made it an explicit faith in the divinity of Christ? There was the parallel between the Annunciation and the revelation of the prophet Sophonias (3:14-17) in which Mary is described as the daughter of Sion in whom the Lord has promised to be present. We might add to this implication the name of the child, Jesus, which means "Lord Savior," by which it was revealed that Mary would have the Lord as son. "In the light of the Scriptures which the angel distinctly refers to in his address, Mary understands that she is the new Israel in whom God is going to abide, and she foresees how this promise is to be fulfilled: through a maternity never before dreamed of which is to bring forth the Lord Himself."[40]

The comparison with the text of Sophonias undeniably shows us that the promise of the enduring presence of the Lord among his people is eminently fulfilled in the Blessed

Virgin at the moment when she became the mother of Christ. But did Mary have any thought of this text as she listened to the words of the angel? Is it likely that she could have instantaneously drawn from this comparison such a stupefying conclusion as the divinity of her son? At that moment she could not engage in a work of exegesis such as might be undertaken today by those who make a detailed analysis of Scripture and are, moreover, in possession of the dogma of the divinity of Christ.

Furthermore, do we not presume upon the gospel text by interpreting it as the annunciation of a motherhood which would have as object the Lord Himself? The child will be called "Jesus," but this does not signify that the child in person is the Lord Savior. It indicates that through this child the Lord will save his people. This name had already been given to others who were mere human beings. Besides, this identification of Jesus with the Lord Savior would not be correct because it would neglect the distinction between the Father and the Son, and would seem to make the divine maternity of Mary a maternity with respect to God the Father and the Son. Now, the message of the angel clearly marks the distinction between Jesus and Yahweh. "Thou shalt call his name Jesus . . . . . and the Lord God will give him the throne of David his father." Jesus is not then identified with the Lord God.

The words, "The Holy Spirit shall come upon thee and the power of the Most High shall overshadow thee," have likewise offered a basis for the argument that Mary understood the revelation of the divinity of Jesus from the angel's message. The expression, "overshadow," had been used expressly in the Old Testament to designate the manner in which the cloud, the symbol of the divine presence, hung over the tabernacle in which the Ark of the Covenant was kept (Exod. 40:35). It was the word, therefore, which characterized the presence of God, especially that which had rested over the tabernacle erected by Moses, and which would still continue in the Temple of Jerusalem. Moreover, it is the word that the Evangelists use in the account of the Transfiguration when, after having described the transformation of Christ, the apparition of Moses and of Elias, and the reaction of the apostles, they state that "there came a cloud and overshadowed them" (Luke 9:34-35; Matt. 18:5; Mark 9:7). This cloud holds the presence of the Father and announces the divine sonship of Jesus, since a voice from the cloud is heard: "This is my beloved son." Father Lyonnet, therefore, recognizes in the sentence, "The power of the Most High shall overshadow thee," a clear indication of the divine presence which was to come down to Mary, and he adds that this indication is the reason for the succeeding verse, "and therefore the Holy One to be born shall be called the Son of God." The use of the names "holy" and "Son of God" is not really justified, he believes, unless the angel has first announced the transcendent presence of God in the womb of the Virgin.[41] Mary was, therefore, making her act of faith in the divinity of Christ when she gave her consent to the angel.

Father Lyonnet gives the following explanation of the very profound meaning of the message: "This divine presence, which had formerly rested over the Tabernacle, had so filled the House as to prevent Moses from entering, then dwelt in the Temple of Jerusalem, or more exactly the most secret part of this Temple, the Holy of holies; this presence which finally was to consecrate the symbolic Temple of the Messianic era, the Angel Gabriel declares to Mary is now coming to pass within her womb, transforming this virginal womb into a sanctuary, a living Holy of holies; this divine Presence which from her infancy she had learned to venerate in one spot on the earth where the high priest alone went once a year on the great day of the Expiation, the Angel Gabriel now tells her she must henceforth adore within herself."[42]

This exegesis has the distinction of bringing to light through its comparison with the Old Testament the full significance of the expression, "overshadow." But could Mary recognize this signification? She had certainly understood that God was going to come to her and conceive within her; but that God wished to dwell in her womb as a babe, she could not have inferred from the words of the angel. Besides, such an inference would not have been correct because the Holy Spirit or the power of the Most High was not going to dwell in Mary as her child. Just as the angel had made a distinction between the child and "the Lord God," he distinguished here between the Holy Spirit and the child. To the Holy Spirit was attributed a transitory operation; and the expression, "to overshadow," could designate a passing manifestation of the divine presence just as in the Transfiguration it will signify a brief manifestation of the presence of the Father. Certainly, the fact of the abiding presence of God in the Temple of Jerusalem would argue for a continuance of the divine presence in Mary, but the message did not contain any clear indication that the Blessed Virgin was to consider the presence of her son in her womb as the equivalent of the divine presence in the

Temple. All that remained very implicit; explicitly she knew of the working of the Holy Spirit to bring about the conception.

The conclusions, therefore, which we must draw from exegetical works on a comparison with the Old Testament are the objective signs in the angel's message that a divine presence would come to dwell in Mary's womb as in the Temple and that the child would respond in the fullest possible measure to the definition hidden in his name "God Savior." But subjectively Mary would not understand the full meaning of these signs until she knew of the divinity of Jesus; they were far too obscure to convey this knowledge.

A similar remark should be made in regard to the other signs given by the angel indicating a certain orientation toward expressing the divinity of Jesus: The child would be great, holy, and would reign forever.[43] He is the Lord who was par excellence great, holy, and king forever; yet, since these attributes of great, holy, and king had been applied to others besides him, we cannot prove conclusively that they were intended to represent Jesus as God. We must first admit the divinity of the Savior before we can fully appreciate these qualities. Mary could find through reflection that these qualities were perfectly applicable to Jesus when she recognized him as the Son of God in the transcendent sense; but she could not, from these qualities, recognize the divinity of Jesus.

If we want to uphold the argument that from the time of the Annunciation, Mary had a clear knowledge of the divinity of Jesus, we would still have to presume a special light because by itself the angel's message did not give sufficient evidence of that truth.[44] In fact, we cannot doubt but that at that moment Mary received light to understand the message; yet, on the other hand, we do not see why that grace would have filled out the message by bringing other truths. There was nothing to be added to the words of the angel, since God had expressed in it all that He willed to make known to Mary and had expressed it in such a way that she could immediately understand by these words all that she should understand. If He had willed to unveil to Mary the greatness of her divine maternity, the angel's message would have granted explicit instruction in regard to it. That message only points out clearly the Messianic dignity of the child and his supernatural conception because it was not according to the divine intentions to reveal the divinity of Christ clearly at the time of the Annunciation.

We know, furthermore, from the incident of the loss of Jesus in the Temple that obscurity in this regard remained in the mind of Mary. She did not understand the answer of her child: "Did you not know that I must be about my Father's business?" (Luke 2:49). The accent is on "my Father," which answers Mary's "thy father." Now, if the Blessed Virgin did not understand the meaning of the reply, is that not a sign that she did not yet thoroughly possess the truth of the divine transcendent filiation of Christ?[45]

It is not surprising that Mary's faith was not fully enlightened at the time of the Annunciation. Anyway, Mary's faith could not at that moment have embraced the whole truth of Christianity because Revelation and redemption had not yet been fulfilled and the angel's message had said nothing of the drama of redemption. God did not as yet ask Mary to believe in the crowning event of the Resurrection of Christ, of which He left her in ignorance. We must, therefore, agree that there was a progress in Mary's faith, which had first been the faith of the Old Testament and would develop simultaneously with the revelation of the New Testament.

Let us try through theological reflection to realize better why the message of the Annunciation was so obscure concerning the divinity of Jesus and why it was necessary that Mary's faith should be developed gradually. In this development we recognize a characteristic of divine pedagogy employed throughout the whole work of Revelation. God does not impart to men the truths He wants to reveal to them altogether and at once. He makes these known little by little so that these truths can penetrate gently and be assimilated correctly. In the Old Testament, we see how God respects the slow evolution of a nation's mentality as well as the law of individual human psychology by which knowledge is enriched only progressively. Since God claims from man some cooperation in the work of Revelation, he accommodates himself to the slowness of its development.

Besides, we wonder if, in Mary's case, it was not desirable for the fulfillment of her duty as mother that the divinity of Jesus should not be made known to her immediately. A revelation of that divinity would undoubtedly have given her a feeling of inhibition and strained the spontaneity of her affection and her motherly attentions. If Mary had to keep telling herself all the time that this child in front of her was God and that he had a right to the homage of adoration due to the Lord, she would have been restrained in her way of treating him and in the intimacy and simplicity of her love. On the contrary, if the divinity of Jesus was given to her as a gradually unfolding mystery, it is precisely in this intimate contact with her child that the Blessed Virgin recognized more and more clearly his hidden identity without being embarrassed in her transports of maternal love. We also understand better why Jesus, at the age of twelve years, enlightens his mother further on his divine sonship and does not hesitate to use words which must startle her. In fact, at that age, he left childhood and like every adolescent, began to detach himself from his mother; this detachment permitted further revelation to Mary of the divine filiation because henceforth she would not need to provide the care which a mother usually gives to her little one and, therefore, she could no longer feel restricted in her mission or maternal instincts.

The knowledge of the divinity of Jesus could be more integrally assimilated by Mary, and penetrate more deeply into her soul because it was the fruit of long, vital contact with her child as well as of contemplation and deep meditation. Knowledge acquired without effect can remain superficial. The act of faith consists not in merely admitting a truth formulated in clear and precise terms, such as those by which the council of Nicea affirmed the divinity of Christ, Son consubstantial with the Father, but also accepting that truth interiorly with a complete submission of one's whole being. Mary had to make an effort to reach a clear knowledge of the divinity of her child but this very effort involved her intellect and body in complete absorption of thought and prayer. In believing this divinity, Mary knew much better what she believed with an inner conviction that she acquired from an intimate association with her child.

The angel's message gave a starting point for Mary's

reflections but did not shed the full light. What basic element in the message directed the development of Mary's faith in the divinity of Jesus? This development could be helped by comparing the message with the Old Testament, particularly with the text of Exodus (40:35) which described the cloud overshadowing the tent of reunion and filling it with the divine presence, or with the prophecy of Sophonias (3:14-17) which announced the presence of the Lord in the midst of his people.[46] But Mary's thoughts could not be developed simply by way of identifying Jesus with the Lord because, as we have noted, the message also indicates a clear distinction between the "Lord God" and the child. The words of the angel who differentiates the function of the child, the function of the "Lord God" who would give to him the throne of David, and the function of the Holy Spirit who was to bring about the conception, introduced Mary to the mystery of the Incarnation only by introducing her simultaneously to the mystery of the Trinity. Furthermore, his sonship of God had been laid down as the starting point of the revelation of the divinity of Christ. Jesus was presented as Son of God by reason of his conception through God Himself.

This was the high point of the angel's communication regarding the identity of the child because, as we have noted, it implicitly contained the truth of the eternal sonship of the Word.

This means that the mystery of the divine sonship of Christ was disclosed to Mary in a half-light through the mystery of her virginal maternity. Consequently, far from inhibiting Mary's maternity, this mystery stressed the capacity Mary possessed as a mother more completely than other women because she alone was the human parent of her child; it prompted her to act as a mother in the fullest sense of the word toward this son. The message of the Annunciation encouraged the Blessed Virgin in an unreserved outpouring of her maternal love. In the depth of her maternal love the divine identity of Christ will begin secretly to disclose itself.

Thus the development of faith in Mary was much more existential than notional, corresponding with the development of her mission as mother and with the ever clearer understanding she got in the experience of living with Jesus and by her own meditation on the angel's message.

Here again, we observe an analogy between Mary and the Church. At the moment of the Annunciation, Mary became the depositary of a mystery which it was her mission to probe, just as the Church will later become the depositary of the entire Christian mystery whose rich content will be entrusted to her for progressive comprehension. Furthermore, it was in the name of the Church that the Virgin was the first to know the mystery revealed by the angel and in the name of the Church she was to make a personal effort to find in it the divinity of Christ. This effort, alone, was to give life and expansion to the faith intended to become that of the Christian world.

SURRENDER

A few considerations in Mary's acceptance still claim our attention. The narrative shows clearly enough that Mary agreed to the proposal of the angel with complete understanding and self-possession. The question: "How shall this happen, since I do not know man?" shows that the Blessed Virgin had regained her composure after the first stirring of emotion, and that she realized very clearly the scope of the message and the difficulties it would involve.

This understanding did not, however, mean that Mary was already aware of all that her Son would be and do. The real identity of Jesus was still shrouded in mystery, nor was mention made of his sorrowful destiny. Mary knew only enough about it to pledge herself; she knew that he was to be called Jesus, Son of God, by virtue of his origin, and that this child would accomplish the work of the Messiah. She agreed to cooperate in this work through her maternity, no matter how it was to be fulfilled.

It is important to emphasize the value of this consent: when Mary agreed to the maternity proposed to her, she accepted it exactly as it had been presented by the angel, that is to say, she consented to cooperate in the foundation of the Messianic salvation by carrying out her role as mother.

Mary gave her consent in an expression of complete submission by calling herself "the handmaid of the Lord." This word *handmaid* connoted an entire subjection to the master. Mary freely acknowledges this subjection, but she does acknowledge it. Her acknowledgment, moreover, offers a clear contrast with the splendor of the royalty of Jesus as it has just been revealed by the angel. The splendor destined for the child will be reflected in his mother, and the Virgin is aware of the honor which has been offered to her; to profess herself to be a handmaid, therefore, is all the more meaningful.

To understand the full implication of Mary's attitude, it

The Mystery of the Annunciation

should be considered in relation to the mystery of the Incarnation as described by Saint Paul: Christ being of the same nature with God, "emptied himself, taking the nature of a slave and being made like unto men" (Phil. 2:7). Now the Incarnation took place at the very moment that Mary, after having been offered the highest of honors, bowed down all the more profoundly to call herself a handmaid. The Blessed Virgin took an attitude characteristic of the act of the Incarnation: this attitude led to the fulfillment of that divine act of abasement. *In the voluntary handmaid is foreshadowed the figure of him who voluntarily makes himself a servant.* The connection between these two attitudes of handmaid and servant shows how completely Mary pledged herself to her maternity and to the mystery of the Incarnation. We may say that the act of the Incarnation is preformed in the mold of her consent.

We know that when Saint Paul spoke of the condition of servant taken by Christ, he did not limit himself to the Incarnation, but was referring to the whole drama of redemption; in making himself "obedient unto death, even to death on the cross," Christ bore the nature of a "servant" to the very end, according to the prophetic oracle contained in the Book of Isaias (Phil. 2:8; Isa. 52:13; 53:12). The Apostle was only explaining a statement of the Savior himself who had spoken of his own death as a "service" performed to the last measure of his devotion: "The Son of Man also has not come to be served but to serve, and to give his life as a ransom for many" (Matt. 20:28; Mark 10:45). If we keep this perspective in mind when we read Mary's answer at the Annunciation, we see that the expression "handmaid of the Lord" forms a prelude not only to the Incarnation but also to the sacrifice of redemption. If this sacrifice is defined by the attitude of him who is a servant unto the end, we can say that it was already to a certain extent in the consent of her who desired to be unreservedly the handmaid of God.

Thus, we see the whole redemptive Incarnation taking shape in the form of acceptance, or more correctly, in the spirit of this redemptive Incarnation. Mary was still ignorant of that whole future, especially the manner of the redemption; she had no special reason for thinking of the prophecy of the "servant of Yahweh" and made no allusion to it. Her answer was very simple, expressing a firm disposition of soul completely in line with the religious sentiments developed throughout the Old Testament. In calling herself the handmaid of the Lord, she did not understand the fullness of meaning that the Holy Spirit, Who acted in her soul before conceiving in her womb, had willed to include in this word. She did not know that she was offering herself as a prefiguration of the Word incarnate and of the Savior crucified, the perfect "servant." But according to the whole plan that has been revealed to us we must recognize this fullness of meaning which had not yet been granted to Mary. The words "handmaid of the Lord" expressed a divine intention asking Mary not only for acceptance but complete conformation of herself to the mystery of the redemptory Incarnation which was going to come to pass through her.

This conformation of her whole being, expressed under the name of handmaid, shows how Mary became mother of Christ *in soul as well as in body*. Christ could resemble her and inherit not only his physical features but, in the deepest recesses of his soul, the obedience of a servant. The personality of the Savior would bear the imprint of the attitude of mind displayed by Mary at the Annunciation.

The narrative does not tell us if it is at that moment that the Incarnation took effect. But the modest desire, "Be it done to me according to thy word," accompanying the departure of the angel, leaves us to suppose that the Incarnation was brought about at that very moment. In fact, only one condition was needed for its accomplishment, the consent of the Virgin. This consent immediately initiated the whole plan of salvation. With good reason, then, may we recognize Mary's answer as a supremely important act, decisive in the history of mankind.

V. Exultation and Thanksgiving

The mystery of the Annunciation is continued and corroborated in that of the Visitation. Certainly Mary's visit to her cousin Elizabeth is inspired by charity and reveals to us an attitude which had no opportunity of expressing itself clearly in the episode of the Annunciation. The Blessed Virgin makes herself the servant of another. But this visit is also a response to the instructions of the angel concerning the favor granted to Elizabeth; the idea of serving another comes spontaneously to the mind of the "handmaid of the Lord." The Visitation seems to be a consequence of the Annunciation; its essential characteristic corresponds with the angel's request. He had greeted Mary with "Rejoice"; we noted the significance of this invitation to Messianic joy. Now the narrative closed with the departure of the angel without our being able to discover how far Mary had responded to this invitation to rejoice. The story of the Visitation shows us the communicative force of the joy which fills Mary as well as the feelings of gratitude which accompany her exultation.

Saint Luke tells us that it was "with haste" that Mary went into the mountains to the city of Juda where Elizabeth lived. The Evangelist was careful to mention this haste in the midst of a narrative steeped in a supernatural atmosphere because it seemed to him characteristic of the special role of Mary in this episode. It would not be enough, then, to explain it by the natural haste people experience when they are going to visit someone whom they have not seen for a rather long time. Mary must have had this feeling; but more fundamentally, the haste resulted from what had taken place at the Annunciation. It is a sign of the happiness that possessed Mary's soul and sought to manifest itself, to communicate itself. It was, in a way, the haste to make possible a *Magnificat,* the impulse of a joy craving for expression.

The description of this journey in haste into the mountains reminds us of the words from the Book of Consolation: "How beautiful upon the mountains are the feet of him that bringeth good tidings and that preacheth peace: of him that showeth forth good, that preacheth salvation, that saith to Sion: Thy God shall reign" (Isa. 52:7). Saint Paul saw a fulfillment of this prophetic passage in the preaching of the apostles (Rom. 10:15).[47] But was not Mary the first to fulfill it? On that journey of the Visitation, was she not the first messenger of good news, the first bearer of "the Gospel?" There is a striking resemblance between the picture sketched briefly by Saint Luke and the figure from the Book of Consolation. The prophet saw the messenger running over the mountains, almost leaping over them, to announce the good news more quickly; likewise, Mary hastens into the mountain country. She goes to Judea as if to say to Sion: "Thy God reigns"; for that is really the substance of the message of the Annunciation, the setting up of the Messianic kingdom by God.

If we remember that the exhortation "Rejoice" was addressed to Mary as holding the place of Sion, we realize that the Virgin performed the part assigned to her; she had received joy in the name of all the people and she is hastening as a messenger desiring to communicate it. This communication takes place at the moment in which she salutes Elizabeth: Elizabeth's child leaps for joy in his mother's womb. In this physical stirring, this leaping of the child in his mother's womb, we can recognize the violence of the Messianic joy as it had been announced by the prophets. The exhortations to "rejoice" addressed to the Jewish people of the Old Testament are now being obeyed by Mary. In fact, immediately after the Blessed Virgin has spilled out her joy, she explains how deeply she is penetrated with it: "My spirit rejoices in God my Savior" (Luke 1:47).

Sometimes the attention of commentators is focused on the sanctification at that moment of Elizabeth's child. But the text brings out something besides this personal sanctification of the infant: the trembling is interpreted by Elizabeth as a trembling of joy provoked by the coming of the Messiah. That is why Elizabeth asks: "And how have I deserved that the mother of My Lord should come to me?" (Luke 1:43). She calls Mary's child "my Lord," according to the expression of Psalm 110 which under this name designated the Messiah established by the Lord in his royal sovereignty. Therefore, it really is *the exultation enkindled by the Messiah,* long predicted in Scripture, that we see in the episode of the Visitation.

Moreover, this joy carries along with it a complete transformation of soul, proven by the fact that "Elizabeth was filled with the Holy Spirit." The coming of the Messiah within Mary communicates a plenitude of grace together with happiness. It diffuses the Holy Spirit; this effusion is an indication of the divinity of the Messiah because his presence gives the divine Spirit. This gift of the plenitude of the Holy Spirit is the gift of the plenitude of the Messianic blessings included in the effusion of the Spirit. Moreover, it is the Messianic salvation with all its spiritual riches that is granted to Elizabeth.

Mary immediately gives tribute to God Himself for this joy; this effusion is her hymn of gratitude, which bursts forth from her lips at the moment, but which had doubtless taken shape in her mind along the way. The transport that made her hasten now impelled her to wonder at God's designs and to give thanks. In her *Magnificat* she responds to the praise which Elizabeth had just given her: "Blessed art thou among women and blessed is the fruit of thy womb!" (Luke 1:42). The Blessed Virgin recognizes the immensity of this benediction by declaring that it is the work of divine Omnipotence.

The whole hymn develops, as its fundamental theme, *the magnificence of God which has poured itself out gratuitously in an adverse proportion to all human rights.* The lowly are exalted and the hungry are filled with good things. Alluding to herself, Mary declares that God has "regarded the humility (lowliness) of his handmaid" (Luke 1:48). This word *humility* has given rise to diverse interpretations.[48] It certainly does not signify the virtue of humility for that is not the meaning of the Greek word; the Blessed Virgin, who gives exclusive praise to God and none to herself, does not attribute to herself the merit of humility. Grammatically, we could translate the Greek word by "humiliation"; some theologians see in it a reference to the vexations of which Mary might have been the victim, to the aversion and hatred which might have been roused in her neighbors because of her privileged greatness and purity.[49] But such an allusion would normally suppose some revengeful satisfaction regarding a situation that had left traces of bitterness; such a sentiment would denote an imperfection of charity in the soul of Mary and must, therefore, be excluded. In fact, the term is to be explained by the actual words of the narrative of the Annunciation itself rather than by conjectures on certain events in the life of Mary. This narrative indicates the lowly condition of Mary, a young girl in an insignificant little village, whence it was said that nothing good could come. Besides, Mary had accepted this lowly condition of her own free will: by her resolution of virginity, she had chosen to be "poor" before God, and to bear the opprobrium of barrenness. It is this condition of human poverty and barrenness that God looked upon. In expressing this idea, the Blessed Virgin repeated a sentence uttered by Anna, the mother of Samuel (I Kings 1:11) and she repeated it to Elizabeth who, like Anna, had suffered a long time from barrenness. By these words, "the humility (lowliness) of his handmaid," she very definitely meant the barrenness of her

[73]

virginal state that made her inferior from a human viewpoint to other women who could become mothers. This particular allusion was suitable to a hymn of gratitude for a miraculous maternity. The Virgin reckoned herself in the group of barren women of the Old Testament to whom the Lord had granted a marvelous fecundity.

In a more general way, she aligned herself with all the "poor," with all the people of lowly condition. And in what had come upon her, she recognized and praised the amazing triumph which God desires to give to them all. In fact, she expresses herself in the name of all people and names the humble and the hungry because she is singing her hymn of thanksgiving to the Lord *in the name of humanity,* just as in the name of humanity she had responded to the angel's invitation to rejoice. In Mary, feeble and impoverished humanity is filled with good things, according to divine mercy.

VI. Silence toward Joseph

Another epilogue of the Annunciation is given us in the Gospel of Saint Matthew. It does not really provide any further light on Mary's personality and behavior. It confirms, above all, the virginal conception of the Savior through the operation of the Holy Spirit by relating how an angel disclosed this truth to Joseph and put an end to his anguish of spirit.

Although the Evangelist does not describe Mary's attitude, what he tells us about Joseph's anxiety helps us to understand the situation. Mary has deliberately refrained from revealing to Joseph what took place at the Annunciation, or even from giving him a hint of this extraordinary divine intervention. Her silence toward her betrothed contrasts with her attitude toward Elizabeth: with her cousin, Mary shares her joy and her thanksgiving. This difference in conduct is a consequence of the angel's message itself; the angel named Elizabeth as an example of a miraculous maternity granted by God and he pointed out her common destiny with Mary: both seem to be enrolled in the same plan of God. This bond of destiny grows stronger from the first moment of their meeting when Elizabeth is filled with the Holy Spirit as she hears the salutation of Mary and recognizes Mary as the mother of the Messiah. It was a clear enough indication from God to let Mary pour out her happiness without danger of indiscretion.

On the contrary, the angel did not mention Joseph although he represented an important element in Mary's future. Was the miraculous conception through the Holy Spirit going to compromise or preserve the marriage? The decision belonged to God; the maintenance of the marriage would present an entirely new interpretation: a paternity in regard to the Messiah that was to be recognized as Joseph's. Only God could confer such a paternity in the measure in which he judged it conformable to his design of salvation. Indeed, the Angel Gabriel had implied in the message of the Annunciation that Joseph would be recognized as the father; thus the marriage would be maintained. In fact, he had announced that the child would occupy the throne "of David, his father" (Luke 1:32). Now it is precisely through Joseph that Jesus is descended from the race of David. Saint Matthew will be careful to note the name applied to Joseph by the angel, "Joseph, son of David," to show how the Messiah belongs to the line of David.[50] But the message of the Annunciation alluded to this merely indirectly, in an obscure way, and Mary must have been impressed by the much more evident and striking fact that there was no mention of Joseph. Was this not a sign that God would arrange his status at the opportune time? This is the explanation for Mary's silence in regard to her betrothed.

We can imagine the whole interior drama which this silence effected in him. Saint Matthew speaks only of Joseph's perplexity and of his idea of breaking the betrothal. Mary must have suffered even more, inasmuch as she was conscious of provoking the crisis by her silence; knowing that one word of explanation would be enough to reassure her betrothed, she realized that the divine will required her not to intervene and to keep the secret. What must have been particularly difficult for Mary, in addition to the prospect of a breaking of the betrothal, was the danger to which she exposed herself of losing her reputation of virginity in the eyes of Joseph. It required an astonishing strength of soul to say nothing, to do nothing but abandon herself to the guidance of God.

It is very important to note that this interior drama was willed by God; it could have been easily avoided by the angel's arrival earlier. We recognize here an intention in the divine plan of basing the union between Mary and Joseph on sacrifice. Before becoming a mother, Mary had renounced maternity by her resolution of virginity; before the final ratification of the marriage, Mary and Joseph must agree to renounce it unless God should intervene. It is actually a renunciation of taking by human means what is to be received supernaturally from God in purity.

Furthermore, if we reflect that it is the coming of the Messiah into the Virgin's womb that causes this drama, we find here the first indication of a salvation that will involve pain, of a drama of redemption. In the Annunciation, the Angel Gabriel had not foretold the painful aspect of the redemption. He presented Jesus as the Messiah King and limited himself to an invitation to rejoice. Now this joy in Mary's soul is accompanied by great moral suffering. Before being warned by divine light of the tragic destiny of the Messiah, Mary experiences the drama that the infant brings into this world, so to speak. The happiness of carrying the Savior within her is purchased by great suffering.

There even seems to be evidence of God's will to intensify this pain because the angel does not appear until the last moment when Joseph is about to commit the irreparable act. It is a preparation for the announcement of the sword of sorrow. After having been chosen to receive the Messianic joy, Mary welcomes the suffering that is inseparable from it.

II

The Mystery of the Presentation in the Temple

I. The departure for Bethlehem and the Birth of Jesus

We shall consider the birth of Jesus in the light of His presentation in the Temple because the circumstances of that event form part of a new stage leading up to the offering of the Messiah in the sanctuary. We have already remarked a striking contrast between the Annunciation and the announcement made to Zachary. Zachary had received the divine message in the Temple, whereas the angel had left the divine presence to carry the good news to the house in Nazareth. We noted that this was a symbol of what occurred at the Incarnation when God came down from Heaven to dwell among men. Now, as soon as the Incarnation has taken place, the journey to Bethlehem and then the presentation of the child show the opposite line of action — a going up to Jerusalem and to the Temple. The Son of God, who had left the Father, is already beginning to go back to the Father. Compare John 16:28: "I came forth from the

Father and have come into the world. Again I leave the world and go to the Father."

The departure for Bethlehem certainly is justified in the divine plan by the Messianic pattern: The child who is destined to occupy "the throne of David his father" will be born in the city of David. And soon after, like David, he will go from Bethlehem to Jerusalem, where the old man Simeon will proclaim him Messiah and Savior and will see in him the glory of the people of Israel. But the circumstances of the departure for Bethlehem and of the birth of Jesus show at the same time an essential characteristic of that Messianic destiny: suffering. The journey to Bethlehem, unlike the visit to Elizabeth, was imposed on the will of Mary by exterior causes; we readily understand that this forced journey was painful to her and upset her plans and preparations for the birth of the child. Unpleasant at the beginning, it was no less painful at the end, according to what we learn from the gospel narrative because Mary found no room in the inn and had to seek refuge in a stable. For the birth of Jesus, God required from his mother the renunciation of her home at Nazareth and complete deprivation.

Mary's maternity was thus marked with sacrifice. It is very evident that it was Mary who suffered most from the circumstances of this birth; she suffered for her child who could not yet offer his suffering. Furthermore, writing of the birth, the Evangelist did not fail to show the positive role of Mary: "And she brought forth her firstborn son, and wrapped him in swaddling clothes, and laid him in a manger, because there was no room for them in the inn." Now this positive role that she plays in giving birth to the child and in the early attentions lavished on the infant, she plays also in the deep significance of the event, in the sacrifice of being destitute and homeless.

If we study this important aspect of the birth of Jesus, we understand better the connection between this episode and the presentation in the Temple. In Bethlehem, Jesus had already taken his mother from her home at Nazareth to lead her to the house of his Father. Carried by Mary, he began to make this going-up to Jerusalem which is to be the crowning point of his public life. It is the Blessed Virgin's privilege to be the first to make this supreme ascent in the name of her son whom she bears within her.

II. The Meaning of the "Purification" of Mary and of the Presentation of Jesus in the Temple

Let us recall the words with which Saint Luke introduces the episode: "And when the days of purification were fulfilled according to the Law of Moses, they took him up to Jerusalem to present him to the Lord as it is written in the Law of the Lord, 'Every male that opens the womb shall be called holy to the Lord' and to offer a sacrifice according to what is said in the Law of the Lord, 'a pair of turtledoves or two young pigeons'" (Luke 2: 22-24).

Three separate times, the Evangelist insists on her conformity to the prescriptions of the law. Consequently, the change made in the legal formula is all the more remarkable. Whereas Leviticus spoke of the woman who had brought a child into the world: "When the days of her purification shall have been accomplished," Saint Luke writes: "When the days of *their* purification."[1] He was not referring to Mary and Joseph, because the father did not contract any legal impurity from the birth of the child and was not himself obliged to submit to any ceremony. Therefore, it is the purification of the Virgin and of Jesus that is meant.

What does this purification signify? According to the modern meaning, it would be a priori rejected for Mary and her child; it might even be said that they are the only human beings who never in their lives had need of purification. We must get the real significance of this purification in the light of the context of the Jewish religion in which it is set, and show what purpose it could have in the case of absolutely pure persons.

The Old Testament held that the mother remained impure for forty days after the birth of a male child; on the fortieth day, she had to go to the Temple to offer there a year-old lamb in holocaust and a young pigeon or a turtle dove in sacrifice for sin. "And if her hand find not sufficiency, and she is not able to offer a lamb," adds Leviticus, "she shall take two turtles, or two young pigeons." Mary was in this latter class: the offering of a couple of turtledoves or two young pigeons is an indication of poverty. The Blessed Virgin could not afford to offer a lamb in holocaust; this human powerlessness of her poverty is fully understood when we realize that, although she was prevented from offering to the Lord a lamb of substitution, she was going to present to Him the true Lamb destined for the lone holocaust that had true efficacy.

Mary could have dispensed herself from the legal prescription because her virginity remained absolutely intact.

But in the eyes of men and of Jewish society, she was considered subject to this prescription. In a spirit of humble respect for the divine will which had dictated these external laws, she wanted to obey them. Interiorly, could she have been acting for some reason other than a simple manifestation of humility and submission? What value did she attribute to this ceremony of purification in her own case? Appropriately, Saint Luke did not designate this ceremony by the technical name (*katharsis*) used by the Septuagint for the purification of the young mother, but a more vague word (*katharismos*) which could mean ransom or expiation. And, as we have noted, he applies the term to both Mary and Jesus, as if he wanted to indicate that the purification of the Virgin was identical with the ransom of her son. He considers the offering of Jesus the most important part of Mary's compliance with the law, because after speaking of "their purification," he calls the action of Mary and of Joseph the presentation of the child. He passes over the aspect of the ceremony which concerns merely the mother. And we may well believe that Mary herself looked upon the whole ceremony according to this way of thinking. She went to the Temple primarily to offer her child and to recognize the sovereign dominion of God over him. Purification for her who was pure meant relinquishing her son by consecrating him to the Most High. This was a much greater offering than the ritual sacrifices of purification.

Actually what was the presentation of the first-born according to the Jewish law? Properly speaking, it was a redemption which was prescribed. From the time when the Lord had struck down the first-born of the Egyptians to procure deliverance for the Jewish people, the first-born

were considered the property of the Lord. They were, therefore, consecrated to the Lord, but since that consecration
was put into practice only by the tribe of Levi, who were
responsible for the exercises of worship, the first-born were
redeemed by a sum of five shekels paid to the priests (Exod.
13:13-16; Num. 3:12-13; 18:15-16).

It is significant that Saint Luke does not speak of redemption of the child but of a *presentation,* that is to say,
a sacrificial offering.[2] His purpose in doing so now is made
clear by the entire redemption which is to follow. But let us
note that this purpose remains perfectly in conformity with
the intention of the legal prescription. When he speaks of
presentation, the Evangelist has in mind the primary purpose of ransom: to ransom the first-born really meant to look
upon them as children consecrated to the Lord. The ransom was the symbol of sacrificial offering. Saint Luke implies that Mary and Joseph wanted to fulfill the legal prescription in this spirit: their intention was not to ransom
but to offer. And this offering is especially meaningful because it takes place in the Temple. The law did not pre-
scribe that the first-born should be carried to the Temple;
the obligation of ransom could be fulfilled anywhere by
payment into the hand of the priest. Mary carries Jesus to
the Temple because she wishes to manifest how completely
she considers her child to be the property of the Lord.

Her action reminds us of Anna, the mother of Samuel;
and it probably had the same effect on the Evangelist because the analogies between the *Magnificat* and the canticle
of Anna were so striking that they could not have escaped
him. Now it was characteristic of the mother of Samuel to
promise that if she obtained the child she desired, she would

consecrate him to God. She fulfilled her promise by taking little Samuel to the Temple to live there in the divine service. "Therefore I also have lent him to the Lord all the days of his life, and he shall be lent to the Lord" (I Kings 1: 28). Of her own accord, Anna went to make a real consecration of her child; it was not to perform the ceremony of ransoming her first-born, but rather a voluntary act which expressed the fundamental truth implied in that ceremonial: the child belonged to God. May we not think that Mary had this same thought in mind? By telling us that Mary and Joseph carried the child to Jerusalem to present him to the Lord, and by recalling the motive that every first-born male child was to be considered consecrated to God, Saint Luke suggests that this was the real meaning of their act: to affirm the unqualified consecration of Jesus; he also was "lent to the Lord" all the days of his life.

Let us sum up the suggestions we get from the narrative in regard to the significance of this visit to the Temple. Normally, the obligatory ceremony which had to take place in the Temple was the purification of the mother of the child. But instead of speaking of the purification of Mary, Saint Luke speaks of "their purification," that of Mary and of Jesus. Apparently he intends to blend the purification of the mother and the ransom of the first-born into one single act and to give greater importance to the offering of Jesus. He defines it as a "presentation" rather than a ransom, and the fact that the presentation takes place in the Temple emphasizes the completeness of the consecration of the child to God.

This must have been Mary's own way of reporting the episode. Therefore, the Virgin must have related the legal ceremony to herself and deliberately sought to make an offering of a child consecrated to the Lord.

III. Simeon's Prophecy

The meeting with Simeon takes place before the so-called presentation, as Saint Luke mentions the fulfillment of the prescriptions of the law by Mary and Joseph after he speaks of Simeon's declaration and the meeting with the prophetess Anna (Luke 2:39). Because Simeon comes into the Temple under the inspiration of the Holy Spirit, his words are preordained to enlighten Mary and Joseph on the significance of what they are doing. It is God's will that the presentation be fulfilled in the light of the perspective opened out by the old man. The coming of Simeon at this moment, therefore, is of more importance than if it had occurred after the ceremony: the same light would of course have been given to Mary, but she would not have been able to incorporate this new light into her offering.

Taking the child into his arms, the old man begins to give thanks to God because it has been granted to him to see the Messiah in whom all his hope has been placed. Not only does he describe the glory of the child without having received any information from Mary, but he describes it in a way which fills out still more what had already been spoken by the angel at the Annunciation: by calling the child "light of revelation to the Gentiles," he emphasizes the universal scope of his Messianic role. In his message, the Angel Gabriel had designated the Messianic glory of Jesus by merely referring to the throne of David, consequently within the framework of Judaism. Simeon goes much further, guided toward universality by the prophecies attributed to Isaias. He borrows his ideas and his words from them: "salvation prepared" (Isa. 52:10), "in the sight of all the Gentiles" (Isaias 43:6), "the light of the Gentiles" (Isa. 42:6 and 49:6). The concept of universality is more striking than in Isaias, because the Gentiles are mentioned before the people of Israel. The inspired old man definitely has in mind all mankind. In his outburst of enthusiasm, his interest centers on the most marvelous aspect of the Messianic salvation: its extension to the whole world.

When we consider this reference to Isaias, we better understand why Simeon follows the announcement of the unique glory of the child with the prophecy that he is destined for suffering. In fact, what distinguishes the Messianic teaching of the Book of Consolation, in addition to its universal scope, is its prediction of the great trials which will bear down on the Messiah himself. The expression "light of the Gentiles" was applied precisely to the "servant of the Lord," and this servant was to fulfill his Messianic role in contradiction and sorrow (Isa. 50:4-9; 52:13; 53:12). The description of the "suffering servant," the most gripping of all those which have been given of the Messiah, must have made an impression on Simeon: if the old man had been enraptured by the magnificent perspective of universal salvation promised to the whole world, he had also understood the tragic destiny of him who was to bring this salvation, a destiny foretold by the opposition which the prophets had met and by the resistance which he, Simeon, could find among a good number of his own contemporaries in regard to what was really required in the worship of the Lord. Therefore, after Simeon has given free rein to his joy in having seen him who is to give light to all the people and to open to them the way of salvation, he changes his tone and announces the tragedy which is being prepared.

Let us recall the words of the gospel narrative: "And Simeon blessed them, and said to Mary his mother, 'Behold, this child is destined for the fall and for the rise of many in Israel, and for a sign that shall be contradicted. And thy own soul a sword shall pierce, that the thoughts of many hearts may be revealed" (Luke 2:34-35).

It seems strange and astonishing at first sight that *the prophecy is addressed to Mary, and to her exclusively.* Ordinarily, we would expect that Simeon would turn at the same time to Joseph and Mary to predict to them the tragic destiny of the child. Apparently, both of them would have been equally interested. Why did the old man speak only to the mother? It is not enough to plead the greater affective sympathy which unites a mother and her child; in fact, simply from the point of view of family bonds, the father would have as much right to be warned about the future of his son because he is responsible for that future and his paternal heart would be deeply sensitive in regard to it.

Simeon's action, therefore, is explained by higher motives: this child is the Messiah. The prophet Isaias had presented the Messiah under the name of Emmanuel and described him as being brought into the world by "the virgin" (Isa. 7:14). Had Simeon recognized in Mary this "virgin" announced by the prophet? Since he had detected the Messiah in the infant, it seems likely. Does he now address his prophecy to Mary because he remembers from Isaias' prophecy the foremost role conferred upon the mother of the Messiah? In the revelation of the prophecy there was no question of a father of the child; only the mother was mentioned and on her fell the duty to give the child the name of Emmanuel which symbolized his whole future mission. In previous cases of the birth of a child predestined by the Lord for a great role, the figure of the mother tended to eclipse that of the father: for instance, it was to the wife of Manoe that the angel had come to announce the birth of Samson (Jud. 13:3),[3] and it was Anna who by her prayer and by her vow had obtained the grace of having a son. In this last example, which we have already pointed out as analagous with Mary's position, the preponderant role of the mother is noted in the narrative because Anna does not accompany her husband when he goes up with all his household to offer the annual sacrifice to the Lord, but she later makes a special visit to the sanctuary to consecrate her child to the divine service (I Kings 1:21-28). The prophecy of Isaias made this predominance of the mother complete because it spoke exclusively of her and passed over in silence the role of the father. Now Scripture inspired Simeon to attribute a like preponderance to Mary particularly because the sight of Mary carrying her child to the Temple might have reminded him of Anna's visit for the purpose of consecrating Samuel.

What is certain is that, in turning exclusively to Mary to utter his prophecy, Simeon wanted to point out that *by a unique right, apart from Joseph, she was to be associated with the sorrowful destiny of the Messiah.* Even if no allusion had been made in the prophecy to the mother's part in the suffering of the son, the simple fact that it was addressed to Mary alone would have been enough to indicate this sharing.

But the old man wishes to announce that participation in definite terms. From the way in which he expresses himself, we feel a deliberate insistence on the suffering of Mary's maternal heart. He could have omitted this allusion and the sentence would have been smoother without it. The grammatical structure, with its parallelism, would have been more regular if the declaration had simply read: "Behold, this child is destined for the fall and for the rise of many in Israel and for a sign that shall be contradicted, that the thoughts of many hearts may be revealed." The words, "And thy own soul a sword shall pierce," interrupt the rhythm of the announcement and seem out of place. These words are just that much more important because their unexpected insertion here shows an intention of stressing them.

The Greek particles which introduce this addition also emphasize its importance. The more exact rendering of the meaning which they express would be to translate "but also."[4] They mark a certain opposition to what precedes, and at the same time an essential connection. It is as if Simeon meant to say: "This prediction of the contradiction to be experienced by the child might seem to be enough; but there is more, you yourself will be afflicted." There is a movement of crescendo in the prophecy, and what concerns Mary represents the culminating point.

Furthermore, we must note the emphasis in "thy own." Simeon had already turned to Mary, because he addresses the whole prophecy to her and he could have said simply, "thy soul." He deliberately emphasizes his expression, "thy own soul" in order to show more clearly how far Mary will be personally engaged in the Messianic drama. As we read this phrase, we imagine the old man looking at the Blessed Virgin more intently as he pronounces this cruel yet inspiring prediction.

The whole figure he uses to express the prediction tends to accentuate its strength. The word which he employs ordinarily signifies the strongest, the most terrible of swords.[5] And that this sword would transpierce Mary's soul means that grief will penetrate her heart's core, grief inexorably caused by the keen sharpness of the sword, grief which pierces the soul through and through.

In this picture, once more we seem to see the influence of the book of Isaias, particularly of the poems of the "servant." In the narrative of the suffering and death of the "servant," we find the sentence: "But he was wounded for our iniquities" (Isa. 53:5).[6] Simeon is inspired by that description of the suffering servant to describe the grief of Mary: like the "servant," she will be transpierced but it will be in her soul. By applying to Our Lady this image which had depicted the tragic fate of the Messiah, the old man reveals what Christian authors will say of Mary on Calvary: she must have suffered in her maternal heart (her *soul*) what Christ suffered in His body.

IV. Importance of the Prophecy in the Plan of Salvation

The essential question of doctrine which the prophecy poses is that of *Mary's collaboration in the redemption*. Is it right to consider the words of Simeon a proof of that cooperation, or rather direct participation of the Blessed

Virgin in the redemption of mankind by the suffering of Calvary?

There is another way of interpreting these words: we could recognize them merely as a simple prediction of the grief which would afflict Mary, as a mother moved by the suffering of her child, but without attaching to this maternal grief any share in the accomplishment of the universal redemption of mankind. In this case, Mary would have co-operated in the acquisition of salvation solely by giving the Savior to the world, but she would not have had any part in that acquisition itself. The sword would resemble that by which any other mother might have been transpierced at the sight of a suffering son.

This belittling interpretation that would reduce the drama which is to tear Mary's soul to an event of private family life, does not seem to take into account all the elements in the text nor the atmosphere of the context. We have already observed that simply from the point of view of family relationship, there was no reason why Simeon would not address Joseph at the same time. He addresses his prophecy exclusively to Mary because he wishes to speak not simply to the mother of a child destined to suffer, but to the mother of the Messiah, since certain passages of Scripture, the prophecy of Isaias and the example of Anna, the mother of Samuel, seemed to associate her more especially with the vocation of her son.

Furthermore, the prediction of the sword is part of the prophetic revelation. It cannot then be considered merely as a word of sympathy for the future sufferings of a mother's heart. The old man is guided by the Holy Spirit in pronouncing the prediction of the sword, as in all the rest of the prophecy; and this higher light is granted him not to develop feelings of natural pity, but to show him the aspects of the divine plan. The sword is part of the prophetic picture because it is to play a role in the drama of salvation.

An analysis of the prediction of the sword and the revelation as a whole, shows that a very strong link implies the close association of Mary in the destiny and work of the Savior.[7] The sword that is to transpierce Mary's soul is the grief caused by the contradiction of which the Messiah will be the object: the mother will suffer from the trial that will afflict her son. It will, therefore, be one trial shared by both, one trial in which they will be inseparably united. The closeness of this association is made more remarkable and emphatic because the old man does not present the compassion of Mary as we usually think of it on Calvary, when we see the mother suffering beside the son. He blends their torment into one because he does not expressly announce the suffering of the Messiah; he predicts the enmity which he will encounter, and of suffering he speaks only of Mary. Consequently, what he sees in the future of the Messiah is the struggle which he is to meet, and in the future of Mary it is the grief which that struggle will cause her. Therefore, rather than announce the passion of the Messiah and the compassion of his mother, he announces the suffering of Mary; and it is through that suffering that we divine that of Christ.

The prophecy, therefore, unites Mary and her child so closely that it reveals the passion of Jesus to us through the sword of sorrow that will pierce the soul of his mother. If the old man had not alluded to this sword, his revelation would not have, strictly speaking, included the drama

of the passion. It would have pointed out the contradiction
to be met by the Messiah, but not the tragic epilogue of
that opposition. The mention of the sword intimates that the
contradiction will end in a drama at a moment of frightful
and complete suffering. Here is the confirmation of the fact
that the prediction of the sword is an essential part of the
revelation. It gives further light on the destiny of the Messiah himself, and it is the climax of what has been said of
the "sign that shall be contradicted." At the moment the
old man deliberately turns to Mary to disclose her future
lot, in the most decisive way, he makes known the sorrowful future of her child.

Why this manner of procedure? Why does Simeon con-
jure up the passion of the Messiah only through the grief
of Mary? It might have seemed more logical to predict the
passion of Jesus with its overflow into the maternal heart of
Mary. But this logic gives a less satisfactory answer to the
concrete situation. It is not Jesus who is coming to offer
himself; he is to be presented to the Lord by his mother.
*Since she is going to make the act of offering in the name
of her son*, it is through her maternal grief that the suffering of Jesus is announced. Mary is thus immediately alerted
to the sacrifice in which her offering involves her.

Another element in the prophecy sets off more sharply
the importance of Mary's suffering in the work of redemption. The prediction of the sword is inserted between the
announcement of the contradictions to come upon the
Messiah and the design of these contradictions according
to the divine plan. The child is destined "for a sign that
shall be contradicted . . . . . . that the thoughts of many
hearts may be revealed." Thus Mary's suffering, which re-

veals the extreme degree of the contradiction to be undergone by the Messiah, is also ordained *for this purpose, the purpose of the work of redemption,* as it is expressed here.

What does this purpose mean: "that the thoughts of many hearts may be revealed"? Different opinions exist among the exegetes on the meaning of these intimate thoughts. Must they be understood exclusively as evil thoughts? Elsewhere in the New Testament, the expression used to designate these thoughts has always a pejorative significance.[8] That is why we are tempted to recognize a disparaging meaning here. In the other passages of the New Testament, the context leaves no doubt; here, on the contrary, the context is indeterminate so the majority of interpreters are inclined to attribute a not yet specified direction to these "thoughts of many hearts:" the thoughts of those who will manifest hostility or those of the partisans of Christ.[9] The contradiction will consequently offer the opportunity of pronouncing themselves for or against the Savior.

This wider interpretation seems better suited to the indetermination of that word, "thoughts," which closes the revelation and is supported by its agreement with the beginning sentence: "Behold this child is destined for the fall and for the rise of many in Israel." Ordinarily, the "thoughts of many hearts" which are to be revealed are the thoughts which accompany the fall or the rise. Before the contradiction of which the Messiah will be the object, some will expose their evil thoughts and will go to their ruin, while others will show their good dispositions and will benefit by the rise, or, in the literal sense, the "resurrection," the passage from death to true life.[10] The fall is mentioned first to concentrate the attention on the opposition to be met by the

Messiah; so it could be that the thoughts from many hearts, while including the two opposing dispositions, mean first of all evil thoughts.

We cannot enter into the problem of the saving will of God in regard to those who are lost; we must be content with merely summarizing the purpose assigned in the prophecy to the Messianic work. The destiny of the Messiah leads men to make a decision that will cause them to gain or to lose salvation. Such is the meaning of the words "that the thoughts of many hearts may be revealed." Now not only the contradiction of the Messiah will provoke our taking sides but also the grief inflicted on Mary, that is to say, the passion of Christ foretold in the sword that pierces Mary's soul. That incident of the passion, the culminating point of the contradiction, plays the most decisive role in the revelation of the thoughts from many hearts. Mary is particularly associated with that decisive phase which is to lead to the fall or to the "resurrection."

Not only does the revelation of Simeon foretell Mary's close association in the sacrifice of redemption, but it is designed to guide Our Lady's life so clearly that it already begins to operate in her what it reveals. Under the effect of this revelation, Mary lives in the constant perspective of sacrifice and she holds herself ready to share in her heart the tragic fate of the Messiah.

After she has heard the words of the old man, she is going to make the act of presentation. The gospel recital does not give us any details of this. It does not tell us what was Mary's reaction to Simeon's prophecy, and immediately it relates another little episode, the meeting with the prophetess Anna. But the very silence of the Evangelist is a sign.

When the old man had saluted the child as a light before the face of all peoples and a glory for the people of Israel, Mary and Joseph "marveled." After the prophecy of a tragic future this marveling is succeeded by a meditative silence. And when Simeon gives the child back to Mary, she understands better the great weight he will place on her heart.

Enlightened by the revelation, the Blessed Virgin then offers her child to the Lord with a clearer understanding of the greatness of the offering. She knows that in consecrating her son, she is presenting him to the terrible destiny that has just been predicted. She is, therefore, offering the Messiah for sacrifice and herself with him for the part which she will have in that sacrifice. In the light of the prophecy, the act of presentation has reached the plenitude of its original significance; the life of the first-born is offered completely to God in view of salvation, as the first-born of old had been held by the Lord as the price of the deliverance of the Jewish people.

After the prophecy has given direction to the act of presentation by giving it more explicitly the nature of a sacrificial offering, it will continue to guide the whole of Mary's task as mother. She knew from the message of the Annunciation that her son would be the Savior; henceforth she knows also that he will fulfill his mission in pain and struggle. Therefore, she will be conscious of advancing with her son toward the supreme moment when the sword of sorrow will do its work. *The whole life of the Blessed Virgin will thus lead toward the final sacrifice.* Consequently, it will be like the life of Christ who came into this world for "this hour." Long before Calvary, Mary's life will be a co-operation in the sacrifice of redemption because it will advance in that perspective. The prophecy might seem very cruel because by predicting to Mary the sword which would transpierce her soul, it already drove that sword into her; but such was the will of God that the motherhood and the life of the Virgin would become a preparation for the sacrifice. Mary was to be coredemptrix for many years before becoming so at the foot of the cross.

Therefore the episode of the presentation of Jesus in the Temple shows clearly the role assigned to Mary in the drama of redemption. It is of the closest association with the Savior in the suffering which is to merit salvation. Mary's suffering is merged in Jesus' and is ordained to the same end: the "rise" or "resurrection" of many, who will be led to reveal the thoughts of their hearts. This association is characterized by a certain priority in time as well as by an ontological dependence. There is temporal priority, because Mary is the first to make the offering of redemption: the act of the presentation takes place thirty years before the tragedy of Golgotha, and yet it is that sacrifice which is already being offered not by the child, but by the mother. On the other hand, there is an *ontological dependence* because Mary is to suffer through her son; her sacrifice will draw all its substance and its *raison d'être* from Christ's sacrifice. The sword to transpierce her comes from the contradiction which will afflict the Messiah. The mother's soul is to be transpierced because the "servant" will be transpierced in expiation for our sins, according to the prophecy from the Book of Isaias that was a preparation for Simeon's. Therefore, the sacrifice of Christ remains the fundamental sacrifice and confers being and value to Mary's sacrifice.

These two aspects, temporal priority and ontological dependence, are justified by her motherhood. As mother, Mary offers her child before he can offer himself; on the other hand, what she offers is her child. It is through that child that her mother's heart is involved in the sacrifice of redemption.

V. The Loss of Jesus in the Temple, Symbolic Fulfillment of the Prophecy

Like the other episodes in the Gospel of the Infancy, the loss of Jesus in the Temple cannot be regarded as a simple incident in his private family life. There is no doubt that it is of importance in the unfolding of the plan of salvation, and that it interests and affects Mary particularly insofar as she is engaged in the carrying out of this plan.

Even more, this episode has a *symbolic value,* for it is provoked by the exceptional attitude of the child. Ordinarily, Jesus "was subject" to Mary and Joseph (Luke 2:51). This submission, which he had observed before the episode, he will later continue to observe. The deviation which he deliberately allows himself on this one occasion is not therefore the beginning of an emancipation but is rather a sign or figure of an emancipation to come. By exempting himself from obedience to his parents, Jesus wants them to understand that he will one day cruelly break away from their affection.

The fact that he wishes to remain *in the Temple* suggests that we associate the episode with the act of presentation which likewise took place in that Temple. The logical conclusion of this act which was intended to consecrate the child to the Lord was that the child belonged completely to the service of God. If we remember Samuel who no more returned into his parents' home after his consecration but remained in the house of God, we must admit that the true dwelling of the consecrated child was the Temple. By letting his parents return home alone and by remaining in the Temple, Jesus was doing only what had been promised in the presentation. His action is the logical conclusion of the offering which his mother had made in his name.

He explains his actions in these words: "How is it that you sought me? Did you not know that I must be about my Father's business?" (Luke 2:49). The translation "in the house of my Father" is a rather free rendering of the Greek expression which signifies literally "in what belongs to my Father" but suggests that it is a dwelling.[11] Now when Jesus asks Mary and Joseph, "Did you not know . . .," he implies a source from which they could have learned or a reason for their knowing. This reason might well be the offering which Mary and Joseph made at the time of the presentation. By virtue of the presentation in the Temple, the child should be in the house of God.

And since the presentation in the Temple, in the light of Simeon's prophecy, had taken on the significance of a sacrificial offering, we are not surprised that the loss of Jesus in the Temple should symbolize and be a prophetic realization of the sacrifice to come. *Its similarity with the drama of Calvary is striking;* Mary is a prey to grief for three days following the disappearance of her son who had withdrawn himself from his mother's affection in his desire to be about his Father's business. This episode, not by words as in Simeon's prophecy but by a prefigurative event, makes Mary understand the threat of the sword which hangs over her and gives her a clearer prospect of the sacrifice of redemption so that from now on, her life is a collaboration in that sacrifice.

Unless we sense this cooperation in the drama of redemption, Jesus' behavior toward his mother would seem too cruel, as the prophecy of Simeon already seemed cruel. But the divine intention was to promote the closest association of Mary in the work of salvation; this justifies the episode.

The loss of Jesus in the Temple gives a supplementary light on an aspect of the drama of redemption not included in Simeon's prediction. It indicates *the denouement of this drama in glory and joy*. The denouement in glory is prefigured by the situation in which Mary finds Jesus in the Temple. "And it came to pass that they found him in the Temple, sitting in the midst of the teachers, listening to them and asking them questions. And all who were listening to him were amazed at his understanding and his answers" (Luke 2:46-47). Jesus has not taken the rank of a master, but that of a disciple, befitting his age of twelve years. Nevertheless, he is in the center of the circle of doctors, and his words are the admiration of them all. In this Temple of Jerusalem, he already appears as one who is mysteriously in possession of the true doctrine and whose superiority the greatest masters must recognize. When Mary finds her son, she sees him for the first time in an exalted position. According to the words of the Evangelist, she is struck with astonishment. These symbolize the future glory of the Master, especially the glory in which Mary will find her risen son.

The denouement takes place in joy. This joy is not expressly mentioned in the narrative but we can well imagine that it was all the more intense because the agony had been keen. In Jesus' answer, we can detect his intention to give this joy to his mother. Still a little out of breath, Mary asks, "Son, why hast thou done so to us? Behold in sorrow thy father and I are seeking thee"[12] (Luke 2:48). And Jesus answers, "How is it that you sought me?" Mary speaks in the present: we are seeking thee. But Jesus throws the search back into the past: "Why *did* you seek me?" He desires to make his mother feel that her sadness is to disappear: she seeks him no longer, she has found him. It is as if he would say that at the moment when she feels sad for having lost him, there comes the secret joy of finding him: happiness is born from the womb of ordeal.

Finally, Jesus' answer adds light not only in regard to his mission and his return to the Father but also in regard to *his own identity as Son of God*. A hint of the mystery of the divine filiation is linked to a suggestion of the mystery of the redemption. Mary and Joseph did not understand what Jesus said. We immediately glimpse the idea that was difficult to them. Mary said, "thy father," and Jesus answers, "my Father," speaking of a different person.

Since Mary does not understand this answer, it will arouse new thoughts within her. After narrating the episode, Saint Luke repeats that Mary kept all these things carefully in her heart. Therefore, she kept as a precious remembrance the words of Jesus: "Did you not know that I must be about my Father's business?" She meditated on their meaning. Speaking thus of his Father, in distinction from Joseph, Jesus had insinuated that God was truly his Father in the real sense, as a man is the father of his child. Mary was to discern more and more clearly that Jesus was in the full sense of the word the Son of God and at the same time she would understand that he must be about the business of the Eternal Father. In penetrating the mystery of the divine filiation, she grew to understand the redemption. Discerning the Son of God more completely, she began to recognize the painful separation which he would inflict on his mother in order to rejoin his Father.

Jesus' response showed the close connection between virginal maternity and cooperation in the redemption. Virginal maternity testified that the child had only God as father, and having only God as father, he was to belong to him completely. There is a correlation between virginal maternity and coredemption, like that which Jesus will declare when he says: "I came forth from the Father . . . . . and go to the Father" (John 16:28). Mary had collaborated in this coming forth from the Father, in the manifestation of the divine filiation of Jesus through temporal generation. Consequently, she collaborates in the return to the Father, that is to say, in the work of redemption.

It was not possible for Mary to see this relationship as we now express it, but her continuous pondering tended to disclose the connection. Saint Luke does not tell us merely that she kept in mind all these events and words of which she had been a witness, but that she pondered them, she put them all together (Luke 2:19). She tried to understand one by means of another and she certainly tried to find the intention of Jesus' words in the Temple by relating them to what the Angel Gabriel had said of the supernatural conception and of the name of Son of God.

The importance of the episode lies in the influence that it exerted over the whole life of Mary at Nazareth. It is an isolated incident, the only extraordinary revelation that Jesus made of himself before the public life, but it gave Mary direction in her relations with Jesus. Since Jesus, far from excusing himself on the plea of misunderstanding, had justified his strange-appearing conduct by a fundamental principle, Mary knew that the little drama of the loss of the child was not an accident but the sign of a destiny. The fundamental principle, "I must be about my Father's business," would henceforth color the life in the family home of Nazareth, which was only a provisional home, not the true home of the child. In that "must" Mary had understood the expression of the inexorable divine will which had inspired Simeon's prophecy. The intimacy between the mother and the son was therefore determined by the nature of the sacrifice of redemption willed by God. She was being prepared for painful separation. The Virgin was conscious of it, and by the foretaste which had been given her, she realized the greatness of the ordeal. The whole maternal task which she fulfilled in the hidden life was thus completely oriented toward the final drama of the redemption.

III

The Mystery of Cana

I. Characteristic Features of the Narrative

The narrative of the miracle of Cana is conspicuous for brevity and simplicity. The very clear style contains few of Saint John's usual expressions and particles.[1] The narrative is free from any insistence on dogma. In the account of the resurrection of Lazarus, Christ himself expresses the chief truth of which the miracle will give witness: "I am the resurrection and the life; he who believes in me, even if he die, shall live . . ." (John 11:25). Here at Cana since no direct lesson in doctrine and no precise symbolism is assigned to the miracle, it has been possible for very divergent opinions to be taken in regard to it. The whole narrative reads as if it has been preserved in its primitive freshness, and as if the author, by conforming to the Master's own discretion and conciseness, wanted to refrain scrupulously from any attempt at interpretation, as well as from any retouching of expression.

This simplicity is all the more striking as it forms a contrast with the sentence that ends the account and that resounds like a declaration of triumph: "this first of his signs

Jesus worked at Cana of Galilee; and he manifested his glory, and his disciples believed in him" (John 2:11). That sentence, which corresponds with the introductory sentence, "The third day a marriage took place at Cana of Galilee," is altogether according to the style of the Evangelist and represents his own comment on the event. It seems as if, now that he has shown restraint in relating the facts, he is eager to point out that in this event, which has been so simply related, there was a manifestation of glory; even more, he emphasizes that this was "the beginning of miracles." This beginning took on particular importance in the eyes of the Evangelist who had expressly begun his Gospel with the sentence: "In the beginning was the Word." The "beginning of miracles" is in a way parallel with this first beginning. In his Prologue, Saint John called attention to the beginning of the glory of Christ, which is eternity itself, and at Cana, he presents to us the beginning of the public manifestation of that glory according to time. In that lies the whole solemnity of the event.

Now in spite of this solemnity, he relates the miracle very simply and very prudently. Moreover, we can well believe that this simplicity is intentional on the part of the author rather than accidental. We get a notion, at least, of a plausible motive which made Saint John especially careful not to add or change anything. This account came primarily from the recollections of Mary herself. Certainly, some disciples of Jesus had been present at the wedding. But it is hardly likely that in the midst of the gaiety of the feast, they would have followed what Mary was doing, the words she spoke to Jesus or to the servants. It is even less probable because these words were spoken in a rather confidential tone.

Furthermore, do we not have the significant avowal that the steward, responsible for the good order of the feast, had not been aware of the incident and did not know whence the wine had come? Evidently, Mary had acted with complete discretion, and only after the miracle did the disciples, informed by the servants, realize what had happened. Mary alone could relate what she said and did on this occasion. Since the account was transmitted by her, it took on a more sacred character; veneration for the mother of Jesus, now the mother of the beloved disciple, would have precluded the slightest modification in the manner of relating the event. That is why we find in these lines the simplicity and tact, the discretion and smiling benevolence of the Virgin.

Furthermore, the narration seems to reflect Mary's point of view, to make known the circumstances of the miracle as she had experienced them: first of all her discovery that the wine had failed, then her appeal to Jesus, her intervention with the servants, her prospect of the operation ordered by Jesus, and finally the observation of the impression made on the chief steward of the feast and the judgment pronounced by him. Mary ended her story here because this judgment had shown her how fully her appeal had been granted. We imagine that she must have related the chief steward's remark with a little smile and by the pleasantry of this *bon mot* concealed the greatness of the event of which she had been the instigator. In fact, by ending her narration with this little tribute to the excellence of the wine, she said, with a touch of humor, what Saint John more solemnly wrote: "Jesus manifested His glory."

There is a valuable guide to its interpretation in this form of narration as it probably came from Mary. Does not the seriousness of the text recommend a similar serious exegesis? Therefore, we will make an effort to respect the complexity inherent in the event, without recourse to far-fetched symbolism to fix the immediate meaning of the words and actions. This respect for the simplicity of the narrative will by no means prevent our delving into its hidden depths.

II. Mary's Petition

MEANING OF THE WORDS: PETITION FOR A MIRACLE

"They have no wine." This manner of addressing Jesus fully reveals Mary's sense of delicacy. She noticed that the wine was going to fail; she visualizes the miserable end of the wedding feast and the confusion of the married couple; she desires to remedy the situation at any cost and knows that her son has power to do so. Yet, in spite of her very lively desire, she merely makes note of the embarrassment and intimates rather than formulates her request. She wishes to leave Jesus free to act; she does not want to submit Jesus to the necessity of pronouncing on an explicit request from his mother. She offers him the chance of refusal if he considers it preferable, for she simply entrusts the situation into his hands.

Nevertheless, in this exposé of the situation which respects Christ's freedom of choice, a true petition is understood: Mary desires Jesus to intervene. The fact that the petition is implicit is no foundation for denying it. If we want to make a point of comparison, we may consider the message that Mary and Martha addressed to Jesus at the time of Lazarus' sickness; that message was in fact a request although, properly speaking, it merely made known the situation: "Lord, behold, he whom thou lovest is sick"[2] (John 11:3). It is exactly the same case at Cana, where the request is directly perceptible in the words: "They have no wine."

It is, therefore, a petition expressed with great discretion. It seems too much to pretend, with Father Braun, that Mary "had made the remark: *'They have no wine,'*[3] in the tone of authority that a mother would use in asking a service of her son." These few words suggest rather that Mary wanted to refrain from anything resembling a command or maternal influence; she does not even voice her own desire, but simply makes known the need of the wedding people.

On the other hand, Mary's action is daring, for she is asking Jesus to intervene with his almighty power. There is no natural means by which Jesus can furnish the wine, and if Mary had hoped for some natural help to save the situation, she would not have turned to her son, but to someone who would have had provision of wine at his disposal and from whom she could expect an act of generosity. Since she addresses Jesus, who has no wine, it is because she relies on an extraordinary supernatural intervention. Her petition is a request for a miracle. Mary had no idea of the kind of miracle, and it would be arbitrary to attribute to her a prevision of the miracle as it was going to be performed. She simply resigned herself to the miraculous power of Jesus. But, in fact, she did appeal to that miraculous power.

OBJECTIONS TO A PETITION FOR A MIRACLE AND
JUSTIFICATION OF THIS PETITION

As the interpretation of Mary's words has been recently widely debated, it is important for us to consider the objections that are raised against a petition for a miracle. Certain exegetes incline toward recognizing in the words of Our Lady only the disclosure of the embarrassment or an appeal for help. According to this, Mary's action would have no religious bearing. Before considering the arguments invoked, let us note that this is the same problem as in the narrative of the Annunciation in regard to her statement, "How shall this happen, since I do not know man?" (Luke 1:34). It is a question of knowing whether we must understand Mary's reaction in a purely natural sense, or if we should interpret it in a context of grace, as an expression of her faith.

The episode of the multiplication of the loaves is given to support the argument that the Blessed Virgin did not expect a miracle.[4] When the apostles made known the need of bread, they simply informed Jesus without having any thought of asking a miracle from him. In like manner, at Cana Mary notes the failure of the wine and tells her son about it; the conclusion is that it is a very natural action which does not signify any petition for a miracle.

It is true that the situations are analogous, but actually the intervention of the apostles takes a different approach from that of the Blessed Virgin. The apostles ask Christ to send the crowd away; Mary, on the contrary, does not desire to end the wedding feast and seeks to avoid having to send the guests away. If the apostles had asked Jesus to distribute bread immediately to the crowd of listeners, they would have asked for a miracle. They did not dream of that; whereas Mary does ask for wine for the continuation of the feast. The comparison brings out the superiority of Mary's attitude, her faith which makes her have recourse to the omnipotence of Jesus instead of considering the breaking-up of the wedding feast.

But is it not unlikely that Mary should ask for a miracle before Jesus had performed a single one? This difficulty has been raised by Father Gaechter[5] and Father Braun. According to the latter author, the supposition that Mary's petition tended to a prodigy "would fit in well enough with the aprocryphal gospels of the childhood of the Savior, according to which Jesus performed miracles during the hidden life. It does not accord with Saint John, for whom the miracle of Cana was the first of all."[6]

It goes without saying that the Virgin was not asking for one of those prodigies that are described by the aprocryphal gospels, of wonderful things performed for pleasure. What interested Mary was not the extraordinary character of the intervention that she was seeking from Jesus, but simply the continuation of the feast that this intervention would assure by relieving the wedding couple from a very embarrassing situation. In speaking to her son, she had not the slightest thought of her own prestige, but of the modest joy of the feast. The object of her request was not the prodigy as such, but assistance and aid.

Nevertheless, this is the root of the objection: since this assistance could not be given except by a miracle, could Mary have had any idea of it, because Christ had not yet manifested his miraculous power during his public life nor during his hidden life had he shown any signs of it, even to his mother? In Nazareth, Jesus had led an ordinary life, far removed from all the fabulous representations that the apocryphal accounts have given us. So, where would Mary get the idea of asking for a miracle? It would be easy to understand that she might have thought of it after Jesus had begun to cure the lepers and to restore sight to the blind, but would it be likely that she would ask for a miracle from one who had never performed any?

Father Gaechter has been still more insistent in his objection against any request for a miracle. From the fact that Mary was one of the pious Jews who were looking for a Messianic salvation of a spiritual order, he concludes that she would not be expecting her son to perform physical prodigies, but a spiritual activity that she was anticipating for the development of his influence.[7] Besides, the fact that until the present there had been no evidence of a miracle on the part of Jesus, the text itself would indicate that Mary would simply have asked her son for help with natural means. In fact she had recourse to the servants, when this recourse would have been unnecessary in case of a miracle.[8] As for the type of natural help that might have been sought by Mary, Father Gaechter believes that she might have thought of the relatives of Jesus, particularly Nathaniel, who was among the disciples and came from Cana and therefore could probably furnish assistance.[9]

But must we accept this interpretation which reduces Mary's action to a very ordinary request for help just like one that any woman might confide to her son? Let us show that the text clearly suggests a request for a miracle and that

Mary's state of mind, far from repudiating it, was predisposed to it.

1. Indications in the Text

Fundamentally the whole narrative implies a petition for a miracle. In the first place, the general aim of the account seems to be to tell us that the first miracle of Christ was performed at the request of his mother. Saint John certainly wishes to point out the role played by Mary. Now it is hard to imagine that the Evangelist would have reported a miracle in answer to a request for natural aid, for in this case Mary would not really have been instigator of the miracle. This is contrary to what Saint John seems to want to teach us.

Furthermore, the response of Jesus: "What wouldst thou have me do, woman? My hour has not yet come," is explained only if Mary wanted to call upon the Messianic power of Jesus and asked him to reveal himself. This response supposes that in Mary's mind the hour had come, and whatever may be the exact meaning attributed to the expression, "my hour," we must agree that it is an important moment in the destiny and the revelation of the Messiah. If Mary had asked Jesus merely to have recourse to one of his relatives, to Nathaniel for instance, she would not have appeared to be opposing the fact that the hour had not yet come.

Mary's attitude after Jesus' reply seems likewise to indicate that her intention is to obtain a miracle. She speaks to the servants not because she is counting on natural assistance, but because it is the servants' duty to serve the wine in whatever way it might be provided. And here, she proves by the nature of her recommendation, that she expects something extraordinary. "Do whatever he tells you," she says as if she were afraid that the servants might be abashed by an order given them, and not seeing how the order will provide the wine, might hesitate to fulfill it. Mary asks them to obey exactly even if they do not understand what they are doing; that is to say, she wants to make sure of their obedience in case Christ desires to make use of them to perform the prodigy. The words, "Whatever he tells you," seem to warn them of something unusual and indicate that Mary is looking for a miracle.[10] Now if she is expecting a miracle at this moment, she must have been expecting it a few moments earlier when she spoke to Jesus. It is certainly not the apparently discouraging answer of her son that would have given birth to this intention or urged Mary to change a request for natural aid into a petition for a miracle. It must even be said that, if Mary had a miracle in mind, she must have been expecting it from the beginning because she had to surmount the obstacle of Jesus' reply in order to persevere in her design.

Note, too, that the recommendation supposes that Mary expects her son to intervene personally, not to seek help from his relatives, because the servants are asked to do what Jesus will tell them.

Consequently, the narrative as a whole as well as in its separate parts, shows us that Mary asked for a miracle and with that in mind she sought Jesus out to tell him, "They have no wine." Anyway, this seems to be the best explanation of her conduct. She turned to Jesus who, naturally speaking, was little able to furnish the steward with a great quantity of wine, precisely because she was hoping for something more than natural help. We must presume that she first tried to find a solution with ordinary means among her relatives or wherever she could get help, and that she soon realized that there was no natural solution available, that there was no natural remedy at the disposal of herself or the wedding couple. She saw, therefore, no alternative but a miraculous intervention by Jesus and she set to work to obtain it.

2. The psychological dispositions of Mary

Would Mary's state of mind have repudiated a petition for a miracle? It is very true that Mary was looking for Messianic salvation in the spiritual sense, but why must we conclude that spiritual salvation necessarily excluded from Mary's mind all material benefits, particularly every miracle in the order of earthly favors? Could not such miracles be a sensible, visible manifestation of spiritual salvation? Was it unlikely that, when Mary thought of the salvation her son was to bring to the world, she also thought of the relief he would bring to people afflicted by corporal infirmities? Later, when the Precursor will send two of his disciples to ask Jesus if he is truly the Messiah, the answer will be precisely an account of the miracles he has performed: "The blind see, the lame walk, the lepers are cleansed, the deaf hear" (Matt. 11:5). Christ cites these facts as signs of his role as the Messiah because they must have been expected and were considered characteristic of the Messianic period. It is natural, then, that Mary should have foreseen that the spiritual mission of her son would be expressed by certain material favors.

For this reason a petition for a miracle is fully in accord with Mary's thinking. Evidently we must admit that this thinking is completely bathed in a supernatural atmosphere because a petition for a miracle comes only from a supernatural outlook. It is a *work of faith*. From this supernatural point of view, what could have been Mary's deficiency or insufficiency, since she had received an exceptional plenitude of grace?

Moreover, the fact that Mary had not yet witnessed any miracle does not in any way prove that she did not wish to ask for one because the essence of faith is not to see and yet to believe. Therein lies the wonderful strength of Mary's faith: she asks for a miracle although Jesus has not yet performed any.

Furthermore, the indications in the Gospel give us some idea of the depth and the development of faith in Mary. At Cana, was not the mother of Jesus mindful of the words of the angel which formed the beginning of faith in her son: "Nothing shall be impossible with God" (Luke 1:37)? Must she not apply that principle to a situation which offered a humanly insoluble problem? It is true, however, that at the moment of the Annunciation the angel had made allusion to the miraculous intervention of God, of the Holy Spirit, and not of Jesus himself, because it regarded his conception. But the angel had also introduced the child as Son of God. And Mary, who from the first moment had believed in her own miraculous maternity, had likewise believed in that mysterious title, the meaning of which she was continually trying to fathom. In the obscurity of the life in Nazareth, where Jesus displayed nothing beyond the aptitudes of a carpenter, this faith continued to develop, her motherly eye penetrating more and more deeply into the invisible which her son was concealing. This searching was sure to find in the countenance of Jesus the reflection of the face of the Father, the image and expression of God, especially after the episode of the loss of the child in the Temple. At Cana, Mary shows that this faith has reached maturity, for she believes that Jesus, by right of being Son, possesses a divine power, like that of the Father, capable of performing a miracle.

Our Lady's course of action bears testimony to a faith which is the *first of all,* in time and in quality. "Blessed are they who have not seen, and yet have believed" (John 20:29). Our Lord's words to Thomas apply exactly to Mary's attitude at the wedding feast of Cana; she had never seen a miracle, but she believed. Her conduct was the exact opposite to that which Christ would deplore: "Unless you see signs and wonders, you do not believe" (John 4:48). This complaint Jesus makes in Cana itself when he is once more passing through that little village. He is evidently reminded of the faith of his mother in that place where it had manifested itself and in comparison is afflicted by the lack of faith that he finds around him. Mary did not wait for signs and wonders to give strength to her faith; on the contrary, her faith had preceded all prodigies. It is because she believed in the Son of God that she had invoked his miraculous power.

There is another question we must answer in order to justify Mary's conduct completely. Why does the Blessed Virgin wait until now to make such a petition since she has always had this faith in the Messiah? At Nazareth, she had never asked Jesus to furnish a miraculous remedy for family privations or difficulties. She had not begged her son to transform stones into bread to help the poor people of the village, and yet she fully believed that he had power to do so. Later, the reason that the inhabitants of Nazareth would give for refusing to believe in Christ would be the fact that they knew his family and that they had never seen anything extraordinary about him. This singularity, which had been intentionally avoided during so many long years, Mary does not fear to request at Cana. What is the reason for this change of attitude on the part of the Blessed Virgin? It comes really from the change in the life of Jesus. At Nazareth, Mary felt that Jesus wanted to conceal his omnipotence, and she respected his will. If the wedding of Cana had taken place some months earlier, she would not have asked for anything. But with the public life, *the period in which Christ willed to reveal himself as Savior had begun.* There was no further obstacle to Mary's asking for that which she had never previously requested, a miracle. Furthermore, she had not sought the occasion but had been brought to it by an unexpected embarrassment. Her love for the poor people urged her to act boldly. Since she realized that she was intervening in the domain of the public works of Christ, she made her request with great discretion to safeguard her son's liberty of action.

THE PETITION FOR A MIRACLE AND SALVATION

Did the petition have a wider objective? Father Robilliard thinks that it did. He maintains that without a doubt Mary, in her kindness, wanted to save the young couple from shame, but that it is impossible to limit her intentions to that because we would be giving a very insignificant meaning to her petition and reducing it almost to a platitude.[11] The words, "They have no wine," have a much wider compass. They recall the prophet Isaias who had compared Israel to a vine, wasted because of sins committed (Isa. 5:1-7; 24:7-13; 63:1-6). Mindful of these revelations of the prophet, Mary thinks of the vine which produces no more wine. At Cana, she has a sense of what is lacking at all wedding feasts, what is lacking in the guilty cities which are the vines of the Lord: "There shall be a crying for wine in the streets; all mirth is forsaken; the joy of the earth is gone away" (Isa. 24:11). The Blessed Virgin, therefore, is addressing the Vintager. "What she is suggesting, what she is asking for is nothing less than the salvation of the world."[12] But the author immediately recoils from such a bold interpretation, and adds that perhaps Mary, moved by the spirit of prophecy, spoke without fully understanding what she was saying. In this case, it would be the solemn answer of Jesus, which otherwise might be taken for a refusal, that revealed to Mary what was implicit in her petition.

Would not such an interpretation deprive the scene of its simplicity and its real strength? It seeks to spare Mary from platitude; but there is no platitude in asking for wine at this wedding to save the married couple from shame and the whole feast from a miserable ending. Furthermore, nothing is mediocre in the charity which prompted Mary to obtain this result. There is nothing in the text to imply that the Virgin was thinking of the prophet Isaias, nor that she is at this moment imploring the salvation of the world. There was no particular reason for asking it at this particular time but the present embarrassment of the wedding couple did constitute a pressing reason for asking for the wine at that moment. And the very fact that it was for a material good adds real grandeur to Mary's petition. The Virgin was not afraid to resort to the miraculous power of Christ to provide enough wine for a wedding because in her maternal love for men she considers nothing insignificant when there is a question of their earthly happiness; anything is worth the trouble of intercession, of recourse to the omnipotence of Jesus. A request to obtain wine is a greater proof of Mary's love than the petition for the salvation of the world.

Does that mean that this salvation is completely absent from Mary's mind? By no means. Mary is asking for material, not spiritual, wine but she realizes that in doing so she is asking her son to reveal his sovereign power, to begin to show his true identity as Messiah and Son of God. Fundamentally, *she is asking Jesus to deign to manifest himself at last as the savior of men, by becoming savior of this wedding through a miracle.* The Blessed Virgin could not have lost sight of this objective because she desired such a manifestation for a long time. She knew from the beginning that his manifestation must take place because the angel had announced it. During the long years of home life at Nazareth, she must have often dreamed of this mission of salvation, saying over and over again in her heart the words of the message of the Annunciation and trying to read in the face of Christ the promise of their realization. But as long as the hidden life lasted, she understood that she must wait, that the time had not yet come when the Messiah would reveal himself to men. The beginning of the public life, on the contrary, gave notice to Mary that her hope would soon be

[119]

realized. Now at Cana the occasion presents itself: a situation that is a surprise even to Mary; the failure of wine that requires an intervention of Jesus. How could the Blessed Virgin refrain from making use of this providential occasion to ask the Savior to reveal himself. She considers that now the hour has come, and as she speaks to her son, she realizes she is requesting a public demonstration of his divine power. And it is precisely because she is conscious of the immense importance of her request that she expresses it with the greatest delicacy.

The wine which she seeks is not salvation; it is the wine needed for the wedding feast; but this wine cannot be given without a revelation of the Savior in a miracle. That is what Mary wants and is asking for.

III. Christ's Answer

Christ's answer raises an important problem. It appears, in fact, to dismiss Mary's request: "What would thou have me do, woman? My hour has not yet come" (John 2:4). Let us analyze one by one the various parts of his answer.

"MY HOUR HAS NOT YET COME."

What hour is meant? According to Saint Augustine, it is the hour of the Passion. According to this interpretation, Christ refuses to recognize Mary at Cana because he is performing a miracle by virtue of his divinity and Mary is not the mother of his divinity. On the cross, he will recognize the motherhood of Mary because he is suffering in virtue of his humanity, of his human infirmity, and because Mary is mother of that humanity, of that infirmity.[13] In saying,

"My hour has not yet come," Jesus is foretelling the hour of Calvary when he will recognize his mother.

This exegesis has been revived by other modern authors, like Father Gaechter[14] and Father Braun. As a basis of his proof, the latter cites the other texts of St. John's Gospel where the hour of Jesus designates the hour of his death. For instance: "No one laid hands on him because his hour had not yet come" (John 7:30); "And no one seized him because his hour had not yet come" (John 8:20); on the eve of the Pasch, Jesus knew "that the hour had come for him to pass out of this world to the Father" (John 13:1). Other passages, too, in which there is a question of the hour refer to the moment of the Passion. Father Braun concludes from this that here, too, Christ is alluding to it. At that moment only, will Jesus recognize his mother. During his public life, he is to be completely and exclusively under the orders of his Father; therefore there is no separation between his mother and him, and the bonds of blood are, as it were, suspended. That is why he bids Mary efface herself. Nevertheless, the separation will cease when his hour will come, on Calvary. By a refusal, Christ implies a promise: the separation demanded today will come to an end on the day of the Passion.[15]

Other exegetes, on the contrary, think that in our narrative, the expression "my hour" designates the hour for a miracle. A preliminary remark is necessary before we determine its meaning by a more profound analysis. When we read the story of the episode, it is certainly not the hour of the Passion that spontaneously comes to our mind in the hour of which Christ speaks. On one hand, there is no indication that the hour of the Passion is intended, and on the other hand, since it is the first miracle Jesus has performed and since Mary's petition was directed to a miracle, we are naturally inclined to relate the words, "my hour," with that event. At first sight, an exegesis which would relate it to another event would seem somewhat artificial. Even if this exegesis relies on texts of the Gospel, it tends to introduce an extrinsic element into the narrative without any immediate support in the context. This observation had been made by Father Lagrange: "To understand in this very simple context 'my hour' as the hour of the Passion, is to sacrifice the thread of thought to a purely verbal relationship."[16] To Father Braun's argument that, if the hour specified the moment for the accomplishment of a miracle, it would be the only case in the Gospel of Saint John in which it would have this meaning, the answer has justifiably been made that, if the hour is to be referred to the Passion, it would be the only case in which its meaning was not determined by the immediate context.[17]

It is really according to the context that we must proceed, for if we run through the uses that Saint John makes of the expression, "the hour comes," we realize that its meaning is determined each time by the sentence and the circumstances. That hour which is coming can be the hour of the suppression of Jewish worship and the setting up of a worship "in spirit and in truth" (John 4:21-23); the hour "when the dead shall hear the voice of the son of God" (John 5:25-28); the hour of the persecution of the apostles. (John 16:2). When it more directly concerns the person of Jesus, it can be the hour when the Master will speak plainly of the Father (John 16:25); the hour when the disciples will leave him alone (John 16:31); it is above all the hour "for him to pass out of this world to the Father" (John 13:1); the hour of the passion (John 12:27); the hour of glorification (John 12:23; 17:1). Twice Saint John makes use of an expression similar to that of Cana, "his hour," in a context where it is a question of arrest: The Jews "wanted therefore to seize him, but no one laid hands on him because his hour had not yet come" (John 7:30; John 8:20).

In all these instances, the hour designates an important moment in the development of the work of salvation. We understand, then, that above all the hour relates to the chief event of that work, the redemptive passion. More exactly still, the hour which dominates the life of Jesus is that of the glorification which comes to pass in the death of the cross: according to the ideas which the Gospel of Saint John gives us, the elevation of Christ on the cross is at the same time an exaltation in glory.[18] The supreme hour consists in that manifestation of the glory which Christ possessed before his coming into this world, the glory of the Son of God (John 17:1-5). Such is pre-eminently the hour, but not exclusively, since the hour can allude to other events. The manifestation of his divine glory by Jesus was made in a decisive way at the time of his death, but it had begun long before. The whole Incarnation is in fact, according to the Fourth Gospel, a manifestation of the glory of the Word (John 1:14), and the miracles of the public life are a sign of it. According to this general view of the hours of which Saint John speaks, we should expect that at the wedding of Cana the expression, "my hour," is connected with the manifestation of Christ's glory, but we are not justified a priori in restricting this manifestation to the single instant of the Passion.

Now that is precisely what the context suggests. We have already noted that the Evangelist considers the miracle the first of the public signs by which Jesus has manifested his glory (John 2:11). This must have been the manifestation of which Christ was thinking when he said, "my hour." Moreover, Jesus was granting Mary's petition, and his words, to be truly a response, must be concerned with the object of the petition. He was, therefore, alluding to the miraculous intervention which his mother was requesting when he said that the moment for such an intervention had not yet come.

By speaking of his hour, he desires to point out that this intervention should not be looked upon as a simple action provoked by circumstances, but as a solemn moment in the manifestation of the Messiah, a moment essentially determined by the Father. Elsewhere, in fact, when Christ speaks of the hour that is coming, he wants to insinuate clearly that the event that is going to take place has been specially ruled and disposed according to the divine plan. The hour for a miracle which is to inaugurate the manifestation of the Messiah forms part of this plan, and it has not yet sounded. Therefore, Christ is complying exactly with Mary's request which looked for a manifestation before the hour fixed by God.

Note that "my hour" does not signify the hour determined by Christ, nor the hour when Christ has all power. It is the hour of Jesus because it is the moment of his glorious manifestation, but like the whole unfolding of the earthly mission of Jesus, it is determined by the Father. If we look for the basic cause, we must say that this moment has been fixed by the Father because it is the Father himself who acts through Jesus, accomplishes his miracles and glorifies him (John 10:37). As the Father is master of the work to be accomplished, he is master of the time when it is to be done. And that is what gives strength to Jesus' objection: Mary's petition conflicts not only with the will of her son, but with the plan established by the Father.

Therefore, it is a question *of the hour for Christ to manifest his omnipotence, the hour for the first miracle*. Must we admit a second meaning? Some writers interpret "my hour" as both the hour of the first miracle and the hour of Christ's death.[19] Schnackenburg distinguishes between the historic meaning that the expression "my hour" has in the conversation with Mary, the hour of the miracle, and the theological meaning that the expression possesses in the eyes of the Evangelist and of the Christian reader, the hour of death and glorification.[20]

We can cite an example of double meaning in the answer that Jesus makes to his "brethren" when they invite him to go up to Jerusalem for the feast of Tabernacles and there manifest his miraculous power. "My time has not yet come," he tells them, and he immediately refers to the hatred with which the world pursues him. Here he means the time for his going to Jerusalem for the celebration of the feast; instead of going now, on the great day, Jesus will not go until later and he will go privately because of the danger which threatens him. But behind the answer is the intention of the final going up to Jerusalem for death and glorification. When he says to his "brethren," "My time has not yet come" (John 8:8), Jesus seems to be looking beyond the simple moment of departing for Judea, for the context gives a broader meaning to his words. They are asking him for a manifestation of glory and, in affirming that his time has not yet come, he cannot be satisfied with designating the time of going to the feast, since that journey, made "privately," will not constitute a manifestation of glory. The time which is yet to come, even after this journey, is that of the final glorification at Jerusalem. The request of the "brethren," now refused, will be satisfied later and in a different way, the way suggested by Jesus when he contrasts the position of his "brethren" whom the world cannot hate and that of himself whom the world hates: The world "hates me because I bear witness concerning it, that its works are evil" (John 7:7). He implies by this that the time of his glorious manifestation is linked with the development of that hatred on the part of the world, that it will result in persecution, and that thereby his glory will be of another kind than that of human ambition.

Can we set up a parallel between these two answers of Jesus, one to his mother and the other to his "brethren,"[21] and recognize likewise a double meaning in the hour of the wedding feast of Cana? The parallel is really not conclusive. The context is different: the "brethren" have made a request which of itself seeks to bring about his final glorification. They urge him to go up to Jerusalem for a feast and there reveal his glory. And the answer of Christ is fully understood only if it is related, beyond the more immediate objective, to the time when he will go up to Jerusalem the last time for his Passion and glorification. At Cana, on the contrary, Mary's request, "They have no wine," evokes nothing like that. The expression, "my hour," given in response to the request, does not seem to have any discernable allusion to any event other than the first miracle. We cannot then see any foundation for a double meaning.

In particular, no theological meaning may be proposed on another basis than the historical meaning because the theological signification of Jesus' words cannot be forged arbitrarily but is to be found in the historical meaning of these words. The Evangelist merely reports the sentence without commentary, without betraying his personal interpretation. If, in his conversation with Mary, Jesus meant by his hour the hour of accomplishing a miracle, there is no more profound theology in that response than what he himself put into it. It is legitimate to separate from it the theological implications and, when we relate the episode with the rest of the Gospel, we should note *that the hour of the first miracle drew in its wake a series of manifestations which would lead up to the final glorification of Jesus*. But we may not superimpose on the meaning intended by Christ another symbolic meaning which would refer to his death. Let us respect the simplicity of the sentence and the implications of the context: "My hour has not yet come" means that the hour for performing the first miracle has not yet sounded and that it is an obstacle to granting Mary's prayer.

If we reflect on the basic principles of this answer and on the plan of the revelation of the Messiah which stood in the way of Mary's petition, we readily understand that the first revelation of the Savior's glory could have been envisaged by the Father in circumstances other than the lack of wine at a marriage feast. The cure of the blind, lepers or paralytics would, for example, have represented a more substantial favor, symbolizing the light that Christ brings into this world, the health and liberation of souls. Of much less importance was a provision of wine for the continuation of a feast; the miracle of Cana is, moreover, the only one of its kind, occupying a unique place among the miracles of Jesus. Later, the miracle of the multiplication of the loaves will respond to the necessity of the hungry crowds, while here in a superfluous way, it is simply a question of prolonging the gaiety of a wedding. At first sight, then, this miracle appears exceptional, strange enough to inaugurate the series of miracles of the Savior; by its very nature, it seems to testify that it was performed at an hour which was not its own.

In the light of the performance of the miracle, Christ's response presents a final difficulty. In fact, the hour which had not come comes immediately, at the moment when Jesus changes the water into wine. To conform the statement of the Master to his conduct, some exegetes have proposed that we see a question in it. Father Boismard interprets it: "Has not my hour yet come?" That is to say, "Do you not know that the hour has come for me to manifest my glory?"[22] Under this form, the answer would signify that the hour had come, that Christ was pointing out this coming as evident, that he would be astonished to see that his mother did not understand.

From the point of view of grammar, this exegesis is possible. Nevertheless, in this case, it would have been more natural for Jesus to say: "Has not my hour come?" rather than, "Has not my hour yet come?" The "not yet" is hardly justified if it is a question which supposes the hour already present.[23] But the more decisive difficulty that this interpretation raises results from the context, from the words that Jesus has just pronounced: "What is it to me and to thee, woman?" These words show opposition and lead us to expect a negative reply. Far from agreeing with Mary that the hour has come and that her request is almost useless because it is so evident that the miracle is going to take place, Jesus quickly offers a rather sharp objection; therefore, the interrogative form does not suit the expression of this cautious attitude which seems like a refusal.

Other authors have tried to soften Jesus' repudiation by making it bear only on a matter of moments: "My hour has not yet come," but let us understand it is going to come soon. Father Ceroke paraphrases it: "I am waiting only for a favorable moment." "There will be a brief delay before the suitable moment arrives."[24] This modification takes away the whole force of Christ's affirmation, for it was not really worthwhile to declare that his hour was not come, if it were to come the minute afterward. Furthermore, why would Jesus set up a short delay and the choice of the favorable moment in opposition to his mother, when it is really going to follow close on Mary's directions to the servants. Really any modification of the statement seems incompatible with the clearly adversative form of the answer: "What wouldst thou have me do?"

There is then no point of escape: according to the words of the Master, the hour of the first manifestation of his glory had not yet come. The difficulty remains of reconciling the action of Christ with this statement. We will face this difficulty later. At least we have not tried to avoid the strength of the declaration and we accept it as it follows from the text and the context.

The detailed analysis shows that the simplest meaning is intended. Besides, the response was given to Mary so that she would understand it. One of the disadvantages of the exegesis of Father Gaechter and Father Braun is that it would make the sentence unintelligible to Mary for she could not have had any suspicion that her son was speaking of the Passion and she could not have failed to understand the words, "My hour has not yet come," as the hour for Jesus to exercise his Messianic power. If that was how Mary was to understand the sentence, should we not interpret it in the same way?

"WHAT IS IT TO ME AND TO THEE?"

Here again, the interpretations differ because certain exegetes have tried to dull the keenness of a remark which at first seems cruel. According to Canon Cadoux, for instance, there is no question of lack of agreement between Mary and Jesus, and we must translate: "What would you have me do, woman?" as "How little it will cost us, me and thee, to give wine for this wedding feast when for my wedding feast, when my hour shall have come, it is the wine of my blood which we must give, I and you."[25] Mgr. Journet has proposed an analogous interpretation but without having recourse to the mention of other wedding feasts: "What is it to me and to thee? You tell me: 'There is no wine.' But, O Woman, these things of worldly concern, however painful may be their sting — what do they matter to me and to thee henceforth? I am going to have to rise to the plane of the things of my Father. And you, too, will have to live on this plane apart and desolate."[26] These two interpretations insist on the close union of Jesus and Mary and place the weight of the question on "What is it?" minimizing the importance of the failure of wine compared with the importance of the work of redemption.

Along the same line, Father Ceroke limits himself to the consideration of the immediate context and thinks that Jesus merely wanted to reassure his mother by making her understand that the embarrassment would be easily relieved: "Of what importance is this misfortune and this anxiety to me and to you, woman?" Mary's charitable heart, filled with maternal sympathy, had been deeply moved by the situation, and it is this anxiety that Christ wants to calm by suggesting that he possesses a means of settling the problem.[27] The importance of the embarrassment, therefore, would be judged ridiculous by Jesus with reference to his own power rather than to the things of the Father or to the sacrifice of redemption.

These interpretations might seem to hold too literally to the words of the Gospel since the verbatim translation which Mgr. Journet gives would be exactly: "What is it to me and to thee?" It is true that such a translation immediately suggests to us: "Of what importance is that to me and to thee?" But in reality it is a question of an Aramaic form of speech of which we find other examples in the gospel narratives: each time that one occurs, it is pronounced by demons or by those possessed, who try to repel Jesus (Matt. 8:29; Mark 1:24; Luke 4:34; 8:28). In the mouth of the demons it can mean only the determination to have nothing in common with Christ. Every example in the Old Testament of the same form of speech bears a similar significance: the refusal to admit anything in common with

the one to whom it is addressed. Thus, when the widow of
Sarepta says to the Prophet Elias, "What have I to do with
thee, thou man of God?" (I Kings 17:18; compare Judges
11:12; II Sam. 16:10; 19:23; II Kings 3:13; 9:18f.; II
Chron. 35:21; Os. 14:1; Jer. 2:18), she declares that she
has nothing in common with the prophet and wants nothing to do with him as she begs him to go away. In principle,
the expression means, "What is there in common between
me and thee?"[28] To recognize in this not a denial but a
proof of close union would be to go against the regular
meaning.

If we want to avoid forming an arbitrary interpretation
that does not adhere closely to the text, we must recognize
that Christ *is denying a certain closeness with his mother*.
Father Lagrange is right in observing that the tone in which
the words were spoken could give them a different color;[29]
but this tone, however gentle and benevolent it might be,
could not substantially change the meaning. It would show
with what sentiments Jesus was animated, but it did not
deprive the sentence of its forcefulness. Therefore Christ
rejected, however gentle and sweet his tone, the idea of
a certain union with Mary.

We say " a certain" union, for it is to be determined according to the context; it would evidently be too much to
claim that Jesus denied all connection, whatever it might
be, with his mother. His sentence is an answer and is understood in relation to the request.

In order to determine the meaning more carefully and
certainly, it is useful to recall the answer Jesus made to the
woman who, lifting up her voice in the crowd, sought to
proclaim the blessedness of his mother: "Rather, blessed are

they who hear the word of God and keep it" (Luke 11:28). Seeing this statement, the modern reader of the Gospel experiences the same impression as in the reading of Jesus' answer at Cana, the impression of a distance which Christ expressly puts between his mother and himself. Intentionally, he does not manifest any approbation of the beautiful touching praise given to his mother by the unknown woman. The blessedness of which this woman has just spoken, he hastens to say, is on a higher plane, in the realm of the execution of the divine will. The reason for his caution is evident: The woman had spontaneously thought that the mother of Christ shared his blessedness, was associated with his glorious destiny. Jesus points out that under the mere title of mother Mary has no claim to this happiness for he has not come to obtain worldly joys for the benefit of his family; the joy which he comes to announce is the higher joy of the kingdom of God, a joy in which we all may participate in the measure that we listen to the divine word. That is why he rejects the idea of a common family bond with Mary and approves only a union of a higher order, a union of accomplishment of the will of the Father. It is only under the title of this higher relationship that his mother can share Messianic blessedness.

It is not surprising, therefore, that at the wedding of Cana, Jesus utters a statement similar to that which, later on, will be suggested by his answer to the woman in the crowd. He resolutely dispels the idea of a favor granted to Mary by virtue of the family bonds which unite him to her. The situation might have made us believe that the intervention of Jesus was due to these ties. Apparently, for some hours at least, Mary had reconstituted the family relationship which she had lived in company with her son for many years. And the favor which she was seeking was just the kind that a housewife would ask as a woman responsible for the well-being of the family. It concerned a matter of provisions. When Christ decided to act, was he not yielding to his filial affection for Mary and to his desire to help his mother in the office of housewife which she had voluntarily assumed at the feast? That is exactly the motive which he distinctly rejects. Mary had no grounds for hope on the basis of family relationship; the home life at Nazareth, where Jesus performed services for his mother, ended with the public life and was not re-established, even momentarily at Cana. "What is it to me and to thee?" Christ emphasizes the distance which now separates him from Mary. The course of his apostolic ministry is not to be regulated according to the desires of his mother but simply follows the sovereign will of the Father. *The hour of his revelation as Messiah cannot be determined by family considerations,* and all the filial love that Jesus bears for his mother will not make him deviate from that line of conduct. This distance is immediately confirmed by the appellation, "Woman."

"WOMAN"

Father Gaechter is correct in stating that among the Greeks, this name "Woman" was never used except out of respect.[30] And the name comes several times from the lips of Jesus, addressed to different women, without ever betraying the slightest trace of disparagement. Christ always puts into it a note of benevolence, sometimes very pronounced: He says "Woman" to the Canaanite when he praises the greatness of her faith (Matt. 15:28); to the Samaritan when he favors her with an important revelation of religious truth (John 4:21); to the woman bowed down with infirmity at the moment when he cures her (Luke 13:12); to the adulterous woman when he frees her from all condemnation (John 8:10); to Mary Magdalen when he asks her the cause of her tears (John 20:13).

There is, therefore, no basis for seeing in this mode of address any intention on the part of Jesus to humble Mary nor to denote the human lowliness of his mother in contrast with his own divine grandeur. Father Leal thought that Jesus' words set up a comparison between the dignity of the Son of God and the much more modest proportions of her who is his mother only according to the flesh.[31] But the expression, "Woman," is not intended to belittle Mary's condition as mere creature; it is an *expression full of respect and benevolence* as is indicated by the examples we have cited.

The use of the word shows us that Jesus said "Woman," with sympathy and in recognition of the dignity of Mary. But, on the other hand, we cannot deny that he substituted this title for that of "Mother" which would have been customary in the relationship between a son and his mother. In this way, he showed his intention *to mark a distance between her and himself* without in any way depreciating Mary's station, and to set a relationship with her on a plane where her title of mother by itself had no efficacy. The appellation quite naturally completed the sentence: "What do you want me to do?" Jesus spoke to Mary as he would have spoken to any woman with whom he was unacquainted, and this circumstance recalls his answer: "Rather blessed are they who hear the word of God . . . . ." by which from a religious point of view, he placed his mother on the same level with other women and with his disciples in general.

Furthermore, Mary could not be mistaken about his mode of addressing her. The difference between "Woman" and "Mother" which she had so often heard from the mouth of Jesus at Nazareth, must be immediately apparent to her and strike her sharply. If Christ had simply refrained from using any title whatsoever, she would have sensed a difference; but he goes further than abstaining from saying, "Mother," and applies another name to her, so that Mary cannot have any doubt of the deliberate intention of her son to take no account of her maternal prerogatives.

Furthermore, we must not forget that Christ waives this title of Mother in order to rise to a higher plane and to consider Mary in the position she is to hold in the framework of his strictly spiritual work. "Woman," from this point of view, therefore, represents a very noble appellation. Father Gaechter considers that this title must have a *Messianic value* because Jesus' declaration, "My hour has not yet come," has a Messianic content and solemnity. Furthermore, Father Gaechter grammatically attaches to this declaration, the title of "Woman," thus breaking the sentence: "What would you have me do? Woman, my hour has not yet come."[32] This association lends a more solid note to the title, "Woman," and sheds more light on its Messianic significance.

But if we must accept the arrangement suggested by Father Gaechter, the grammatical connection of "Woman" with what follows seems less in keeping with the response. Certainly, in other instances, the title "Woman" used by

Jesus, precedes the sentence which he pronounces. But there is one case where this appellation follows and it is precisely the case where the title, "Woman" takes on a solemn meaning. Jesus, as the Messiah, says to the Samaritan woman, "Believe me, woman, the hour is coming when neither on this mountain nor in Jerusalem will you worship the Father" (John 4:21). He makes the title "Woman" more solemn by placing it after "Believe me." The sentence forms a remarkable parallel with that of Cana where Christ, likewise, wants to give a solemn sound to the title "Woman." According to this parallel, Jesus first says: "What do you want me to do, woman?" Then he utters the Messianic declaration which he has just prepared: "My hour has not yet come." Furthermore, we have already shown that from the point of view of meaning, "Woman" completes "What is it to me and to thee?"

The great solemnity of the word, "Woman," clearly indicates a Messianic orientation. Christ rejects the idea of family union with his mother in his quality of Messiah. It is the Messiah who calls Mary, "Woman," and consequently gives this word its Messianic context. It is not a valid objection that all other occasions when Jesus used the name "Woman" must also take on a Messianic importance or that such an interpretation is impossible, because Mary's case was unique and its Messianic quality was that the title of "Woman" was a substitute for that of "Mother." Other women would naturally be called "Woman" by Jesus according to custom, and no special value is to be attributed to the appellation. Mary, on the contrary, naturally and according to custom would not be called "Woman" and for this reason the name has a special importance determined by the Messianic context.

Nevertheless, we must make a restriction here. It is only implicitly, in a veiled way, that Jesus gave the word "Woman" this Messianic significance. What first appeared in this title was the desire not to consider Mary under the title of mother. This is the meaning that Mary must have derived from it: a negative signification.

Mary likewise must have noted a mysterious solemnity in the expression, hidden under the simplicity of the word. She suspected that Jesus had a broader intention when he made use of this name, but she could not have seen exactly what it was. Moreover, we must speak of the Messianic orientation in the mind of Christ rather than a Messianic expression clearly enunciated. This orientation can be trans-lated thus: Jesus, acting as Messiah, will have only Messianic relations and no familial relationship with his mother; to determine these relationships he recognizes Mary as a "woman" in regard to the Messiah. This position was unique for, although other women were by nature "woman" in the mind of Jesus, Mary was woman to him only on the Messianic plane, above her own individual title of mother.

To gain a better understanding and proof of this Mes-sianic intention included in the expression, "Woman," we must remember that from the beginning of the public life, Jesus applied to himself a title outwardly similar in form, that of "Son of man." By this expression, he seems to call himself an ordinary man; yet he assumes this quality of man by a unique title, the title of Messiah and Son of God.[33] Similarly, he applies to Mary from the beginning of the public life, the name of "Woman" which seems to place

Mary in the common rank of all women but in reality gives recognition to her unique position.

It is evident that the Master has a similar intention in the use of both these names. In calling himself "Son of man," Jesus voluntarily relinquishes the popular Messianic title, "Son of David," which others bestow on him but which we never find on his lips. He wants to show by this that his Messiahship extends beyond his racial membership and is established on a universal plane of humanity.[34] By calling Mary "Woman," he has the same express intention of recognizing her on a plane superior to that of the ties of carnal descent that attach him to her.

Jesus, of course, does not use the title, "Son of Man," at the wedding of Cana; but this title would have perfectly fitted into his statement regarding the hour of the Messiah which had not yet come, and his way of acting seems truly characteristic of the Son of man. Jesus' attitude toward Mary could be defined as *declining to be a son to his mother in order to be the Son of man to woman.*

IMPLICATION OF THE ANSWER

Now that we have analyzed the elements of the response, we may determine their implication. First we must exclude any intention on the part of Christ to reproach or blame his mother. This opinion would be without foundation in the text because none of the elements of the response contain any disapprobation. We have pointed out that while Jesus desired to mark the distance separating him from his mother in the public life, he injects a note of honor and respect in the name, "Woman."

From the viewpoint of doctrine, too, blame would be incompatible with the absolute sanctity of Mary; this sanctity, as it is recognized by the Church today, implies that the Blessed Virgin never in fact merited divine reprobation for her conduct in act or in word. Therefore, we cannot agree with Saint Ireneaus[35] that there was a reprimand for intemperate haste, or even less for a desire of vanity, according to the interpretation of Saint John Chrysostom.[36] These opinions were expressed at a time when the Church had not yet clearly understood the implications of Mary's sanctity.[37]

But could we interpret the response as a refusal? Saint Augustine, it must be remembered, maintained that Jesus would not recognize Mary because she was not the mother of his divinity, but only of his human nature. Such an objection is too strong for the text because, as we have mentioned, Jesus does not desire by the name of "Woman" to belittle his mother nor to contrast his own divine dignity with the much more modest situation of Mary as mother according to the flesh. We have even added that, quite the contrary, by this appellation, Christ raises the position of his mother to the level of Messianic activity.

A comparison with the brethren of Jesus is used to prove that a refusal is intended.[38] Christ rejected his mother's request at Cana as he will later reject the invitation to go up to Jerusalem and manifest his glory by a more open journey. If in both cases he appears to do afterwards what he has been asked, this is only an appearance that veils a real refusal, founded on the principle that in his public life Jesus does not take account of the bonds of blood and governs his actions only according to the designs of his Father.[39]

We lose sight of the fact that the two requests spring

from fundamentally different inspirations: the brethren of Jesus are impelled by their incredulity and their vanity while Mary is led by her faith and a humility that is entirely subject to the divine will. Christ's reaction, moreover, far from being identical in the two cases, differs according to the two attitudes. Jesus really refuses his brethren and he does not retract nor derogate from the motive of his refusal because he does not go to Jerusalem in a public ostensible way. In that refusal he simply implies that one day the manifestation of his glory in Jerusalem which his brethren have in mind will take place but in a manner completely different from their ambitious dreams. At Cana, on the contrary, he fulfills Mary's desire, not only in appearance but in fact, through the concrete reality of the miracle. We must, then, distinguish carefully between his refusal to yield to the demands of his brethren for the manifestation of prodigies and his response to Mary's request for a miracle.

In Mary's petition, there was nothing inordinate, which would have deserved a refusal. Will some one say that at the wedding of Cana there was a temptation for the Blessed Virgin? Some see here a parallel to Jesus' temptation in the desert. Satan had suggested to Jesus to perform a miracle by changing stones into bread; at Cana, Mary is tempted to ask for a miracle and transmits the temptation to her Son. Jesus repels the temptation by a refusal which is addressed not to his mother, but to the tempter.[40] Such an interpretation supposes that Mary, by appealing to Jesus of her own volition, has made herself the instrument of a diabolic temptation. How could we admit such an eventuality which would make recognizable to Christ in the words, "They have no wine," the very voice of Satan? More inexplicable still would be the conclusion that, unlike his attitude toward the temptation in the desert where he had refused to change stones into bread, Jesus would have yielded to the suggestion of Satan and transformed the water into wine. Mary cannot be shown as spokesman of a diabolic temptation.

In the narrative itself, two indications clearly oppose any attempt to interpret the response of Jesus as a refusal. First, Mary persevered in her intention to obtain a miracle, as is proved by her directions to the servants. Now, if she had seen in the words of her son any sign of not receiving what she asked, she would not have persisted in her intention, first because she would have realized that all insistence would be futile and secondly, because she would have refrained from resisting the will of Jesus speaking as Messiah. Mary was, in fact, completely docile to the designs of God. She perseveres because she understands the response otherwise than as a refusal. She thinks that a possibility of succeeding remains open to her.

The second proof is that Christ performs the miracle Mary requests. There is no contradiction between this act and the words which have just been uttered. If Jesus grants his mother's request, he did not a minute before intend to refuse her. We cannot pretend that, after having set up the principle that his mother must not intervene in the affairs of his public life, Christ derogates from this principle and allows an exception which is the miracle,[41] because there could be no derogation from this principle formed by Christ, and the miracle is not an exemption. Mary certainly obtained the first miracle, but this influence was not due to her own special right as mother of Jesus. The rule, therefore, was respected by the action of Christ.

Let us note that the theory of a temporary refusal meets an additional difficulty when it supposes that the principle formulated by Jesus is valid only at the time of the Passion. Between Cana and then, Mary could not intervene in her capacity as a mother, but once the hour of Calvary had come, she would resume her title to maternal intervention in the work of salvation. In fact, even on Calvary, Jesus will not say to Mary, "Mother" but "Woman" and will show by that that he is not departing from the attitude taken in regard to her at Cana. Mary's role in the Messianic work is definitely not determined by the private title of mother, and the simple ties of blood would not justify her action in that higher realm.

In affirming this principle, there was no refusal but an *objection*. Or, if there was a refusal, this refusal was limited to an influence of a certain type. Now, in fact, Mary was well aware that she was intervening in an area where her authority as mother had no right of command. She knew that the intimacy of Nazareth no longer ruled the life of her son and that, in the accomplishment of his mission as Savior, Jesus was going to take no account of familial interests. She knew it so well that at Cana her relations with her son spontaneously assume a higher level: she, who heretofore had never asked Jesus for a miracle, now asks him for one. Thus she rises to the level of the public life and of the Messianic revelation of Christ. Furthermore, for this reason she presents her request with great delicacy and as a mere suggestion. She feels, in fact, that she is going beyond her strict mission as mother, which concerned only the private person of Jesus. Therefore, the response must not have surprised Mary very much because the objection made by Jesus showed more clearly what she herself had anticipated.

By refusing to be influenced by Mary merely as his mother, Jesus did not reject every overture on her part because a possibility was left to her to act under the title of "Woman." But it is precisely here on this Messianic level where Mary could act only as woman, that the obstacle arises: the hour fixed by the Father had not yet come. It was a considerable obstacle, evidently, since it was a question of a divine ordinance. If Christ had presented this obstacle as insurmountable, his answer would have been a refusal. But did he make the obstacle conclusive? By her conduct, Mary shows that she did not understand it as conclusive, and by his demeanor Christ is going to approve the manner in which his mother understood his response and reveal that evidently the obstacle could be surmounted.

Finally another consideration has been invoked to prove that Jesus' words signified a refusal: Mary did not understand the meaning of these words and this would explain her persistence in asking for the refused favor.[42] Such an explanation is mere supposition because the narrative makes no mention of any misunderstanding. In relating the loss of the child in the temple, Mary made it clear that she had not understood the answer of Jesus, but in relating the miracle of Cana, she did not say so. It does not seem, according to the narrative, that she was troubled or disturbed by her son's statement. On the contrary, we get the impression that she does not stop to think about that answer. She acts without delay like someone who is master of the situation; there is not the slightest sign of hesitation.

Of course, we do not pretend that Mary understood

immediately all the implications contained in the words of Jesus. Later she meditated upon these words and must have understood their import more completely. But essentially, she discerned the meaning immediately and correctly. We have a strong proof of this. If Mary had interpreted the statement erroneously and had persevered in her request with this motive, Jesus could not have confirmed her error by listening to her request. The fulfillment of the miracle supposes an approbation of Mary's attitude in both the manner in which she had understood the words pronounced by the Master and the hidden intention which animated them.

IV. Mary's Directions to the Servants

First, let us remember that the exact meaning of Mary's words is not "Do everything he tells you," but "Do whatever he tells you." Nor could we translate it, "If he tells you to do something, do it."[43] This translation would imply that Mary expresses a doubt, an uncertainty, in regard to the actual fact of Jesus' intervention. Grammatically, this translation does not correspond with the text. The text does not begin with a conditional clause, but with a relative clause which is somewhat indeterminate; the uncertainty does not relate to the fact of knowing whether Jesus is going to say something, but what he is going to say. We could translate it, "What he tells you to do, whatever it may be, do." Mary speaks as if she is confident that Jesus is going to say something but without knowing exactly what it will be.

We have already observed that such a recommendation given to the servants shows that Mary was expecting a miracle. However strange Jesus' orders might be and how inefficacious they might seem in procuring the wine, she counseled the servants to obey.

We must, therefore, maintain that Mary did not recoil before the obstacle that Jesus had set up against her. She does not show the slightest sign of doubt or hesitation. She acts and speaks as if she were certain of the miracle.

Yet she is careful not to encroach on the sovereignty of the Messiah. She even emphasizes a delicacy and discretion. She refrains from insisting on speaking again to Jesus, as if she desires to respect his freedom of action even more. She does not cling to him in supplication, as other women will do later, although with success. It is because she wishes to conform to the response which has just been made by him. Since Jesus called her "Woman," she will not yield to her maternal instinct which urges her to cling to her child. Since Christ has emphasized the distance which separates him from her, she does not draw near to him. It is from a distance, by addressing the servants, that she makes known the perseverance of her desire. By the words, "Whatever he tells you," she intentionally leaves the field free to the sovereignty of her son. In this way she shows her docile trust in that sovereignty. When she counsels the servants to be absolutely obedient, it is her own obedience that she expresses and would like to communicate to them. Mary never borders on presumption; her attitude is that of complete submission, of extremely delicate respect for the will of Christ.

On the other hand, the assurance she shows in asking for a miracle is made even more remarkable. Now, in fact, she is preparing the servants for orders which Jesus is going to give them. Thus she leads them to expect a miracle as if she knew it was to be performed. We may say, then, that

Christ's answer, far from turning her away from her plans, only provoked a step forward in the same direction.

On what did this assurance rest? We might think that it proceeds from the conviction that Jesus, in spite of an apparent opposition, will end by yielding to his mother's desire, by letting his filial heart speak. But that could not be Mary's thought because she had understood the seriousness of Jesus' opposition to every intervention of his mother in his public life. She had understood that her son would not go back on this principle, and that if he acted, it would not be by virtue of any merely filial affection.

We could also explain Mary's attitude by saying that she understood the compassionate heart of Jesus; she could realize that he was too kind to leave these people to their embarrassment and, by his own refraining, condemn the wedding feast to a pitiful and inglorious ending. But this motive for hope would not have been sufficient, because the obstacle raised by Jesus was of a much loftier nature: the hour determined by the Father. How would Mary count on overcoming this obstacle?

It was not by purely human or sentimental considerations, by appealing to the pity that a human heart experiences in difficult situations, that she hoped to attain her end. Since Christ had entered the field of his strictly religious and Messianic activity, it is in his religious attitude that Mary found a loophole. Her son had objected that it was against the divine will. But she knew also the strength of prayer and knew that a human being can obtain from God what he desires. Did not the Old Testament offer examples of divine decisions that had been conformed to the supplications of men? Had not God, for instance, shown himself disposed to yield to the prayer of Abraham in favor of Sodom (Gen. 18:16-33)? Mary judged then that, if she persevered in her demand, she could obtain satisfaction; she was confident that she would finally be heard.

We can compare the attitude of the Canaanite woman with this reaction of Mary. She will be confronted by Christ with the divine will that hinders the fulfillment of the miracle: "I was not sent except to the lost sheep of the house of Israel." She will not be deterred by this declaration that would have seemed to exclude all possibility of granting the favor she was seeking. Not only will she surmount the obstacle and obtain the miracle but she will reap praise: "O woman, great is thy faith! Let it be done to thee as thou wilt." Christ will attribute the victory to the faith or confidence of this woman. The case of the centurion will be similar; he too is a stranger and does not belong among the sheep of the house of Israel, but his faith will win a miracle for him.

Surely Mary had at least the faith and confidence of the Canaanite or centurion. She was the first one who looked upon the barrier set up by Christ as not impassable. If the hour had not yet come, she hoped that God would listen to her supplication and that the hour would come. Even more, her faith had a lucidity superior to all others. It was a faith in the divinity of Jesus. In fact, Mary's directions to the servants suppose that she recognized in her son the absolute power to arrange the course of his public life. Jesus alluded to the divine will, to the plan established by the Father, when he declared that his hour had not yet come. At that moment, Mary does not begin to implore Yahweh for an advancement of the hour. In Jesus she places her faith and

[148]

her trust: "Do whatever he tells you." She acts as if Jesus shared sovereignty over his Messianic work with Yahweh, the Father, and could himself decide, in agreement with the Father, the advancement of the hour. She, therefore, attributed to her son a divine power equal to that of the Father and common with his.

We may add that the clue in the words spoken to the servants tends to confirm what the first request already suggested: in turning to her son to ask for the miracle, Mary seemed to understand that Jesus had the power in himself to perform one, acting in his own name. What is in fact characteristic of divine omnipotence is not the power simply to perform a miracle because Peter, for example, will accomplish one later in the name of Jesus (Acts 3:1). It is Christ's power to act in his own name through his own sovereignty. Mary's initial request seemed to rely on such power and to imply faith in the divinity of Christ. The direction given to the servants reveals that faith more explicitly, since she recognizes Jesus' power to change the hour, the power of a divine will common with that of the Father. The prayer of Cana is, therefore, founded on a firm faith in the divinity of Christ. Mary testifies in that emergency that she has truly discovered the fullness of the Son of God in Jesus who has received everything from the Father and is like to him.

Thus we can account for Mary's anticipation that the compassionate heart of Jesus, moved by the need of the moment, will not refuse the favor she requests. She trusts in Jesus, not only for his human bounty, but for his divine bounty which will match his divine power. Mary firmly hopes that, as Son of God, Jesus will exercise the goodness

[149]

of God himself, a goodness which grants requests presented with faith. Mary's attitude at Cana is essentially a theological attitude, resorting to the Son of God and invoking his divine power and goodness.

This is the attitude that Christ ratifies solemnly and without delay, by the accomplishment of the miracle. He advances the hour which had not yet come and proves Mary right in having persevered in her resolute confidence, in spite of the obstacle which he had set up against her. What the mother could not obtain through filial affection, the woman obtains through the divine goodness in which she has manifested her faith.

V. The Theological Meaning of the Episode

THE FUNDAMENTAL MEANING OF THE NARRATIVE ITSELF

The story of the wedding feast at Cana first brings to light a *close rapport between Mary and Christ*. We might have thought that this relationship would be limited to the period of the hidden life at Nazareth and that Mary's influence over her son would have practically ceased with the opening of the public life. This episode shows, on the contrary, that this influence of Mary is still being exercised over the apostolic ministry of the Messiah to the extent of instigating the first miracle, the first manifestation of the power of the Savior.

The details of the event indicate very clearly the greatness of that influence. Mary begins asking for a miracle from him who had not yet performed any. Jesus expressly declares that the first miracle has been foreseen for another time; he could not have offered a more pressing objection than that of the will of his Father who had chosen a different hour. His objection only makes more evident the efficacy of Mary's intercession in obtaining a change of the hour. The effect is so surprising that many modern exegetes refuse to accept it or recognize the hour of which Jesus speaks as the hour of the first miracle which has been changed. But we have shown that this meaning, which is moreover the simplest, must be accepted. If Mary had not acted at Cana, the first miracle would have taken place somewhere else and in other circumstances.

It may seem surprising that God allowed Mary to determine the hour, the setting, and the nature of the first miracle and it may seem that too much discretion was left to the intercession of the mother of Jesus. We have already pointed out that the wedding feast of Cana did not at first sight seem to be an ideal setting for the primary manifestation of the glory of the Messiah. We might have visualized more important miracles because the favor requested was not of primordial necessity and it seemed bold to want to subordinate the beginning of a great religious revelation to the gaiety of a feast. All these unfavorable features only go to prove still more firmly the reality of the influence exercised by Mary, and prove that no scenario was set up in advance and put into place by God; it is truly the prayer of Mary that determined the choice of this improvised setting.

Furthermore, the choice is not arbitrary. In reality, the favor requested was well suited to the manner in which Christ wanted to appear to men. In contrast with the Precursor, whose austerity was the admiration of the people, Jesus comes as one who does not refuse to eat and drink, to sit at table, even with those who are considered sinners.

Although he praises John the Baptist for his high moral standards, he does not himself live austerely; he desires to manifest to men his sympathy and his generosity rather than impress them with his severe penances (Matt. 11:18-19; Luke 7:33-34). The miracle suggested by Mary tends similarly in that direction; therefore, the Blessed Virgin's intercession represents an appropriate collaboration. By requesting wine for the wedding feast, she asks Jesus to manifest himself as he is and wishes to be, in his profound benevolence and sympathetic concern for everyone, especially the poor and lowly. The whole conduct of Christ during the public life will be aimed at revealing divine love. Mary has realized instantaneously that the wedding feast of Cana would be a brilliant setting for that divine bounty toward the humble. Thus she contributes to the authentic orientation of the manifestation of the Messiah.

Here we see the reason for that role left to Mary at the beginning of the public life. The Blessed Virgin is the one who knows Jesus in an eminent way even to his divine depths and is qualified to collaborate with him. At this moment, she alone is capable of such collaboration; in asking for the miracle, she is guided by what she knows of Christ so that her intervention is fully justified.

How is this collaboration of Mary to be defined theologically? Up to this time, Mary had collaborated in the personal formation of the Savior, in his generation and education. At Cana, there was *a collaboration in the Messianic work itself,* and no longer merely in the preparation of that work. In terms of modern theology, it is not enough to say that the episode is the proof of Mary's power of intercession in the dispensation of graces, in what is called the subjective redemption. The granting of the wine is more than a grace dispensed at the request of the Blessed Virgin; it is a miracle by which Christ reveals himself as Savior. Therefore, like the whole Messianic program of the public life, it forms an essential part of the objective redemption. Consequently, it is with this subjective redemption that Mary is associated. Furthermore, let us note she is associated with it directly and not merely in an indirect manner as the mother of the Savior. This prerogative would place her at the origin of the work of salvation but would not imply her immediate co-operation in that work. Jesus himself declares that her intercession at Cana exceeds her strictly maternal mission and through his miracle consecrates Mary's immediate collaboration in the manifestation of the Messiah and the work of salvation.

This collaboration is granted her under the form of *initiative*. As at the time of the Annunciation Mary's consent had to precede the Incarnation of the Son of God, and as at the presentation of Jesus in the temple Mary's offering came before the oblation of Calvary, the step taken by the Blessed Virgin leads to the first miracle. At Cana, this initiating role is more conspicuous because Mary has to struggle for the success of her project. That is the whole importance of that role.

But on the other hand, this function of initiative does not by any means confer first rank on Mary. Christ remains at the center of the scene. We have already noted that the Virgin regulates her conduct precisely on what she knows of Christ so that Christ is the real foundation of her petition. Her intercession has likewise been focused on Christ, whose glorious manifestation she desires. In fact, the whole scene converges toward the glory of Jesus, mentioned by Saint John at the end of his Gospel. One of the difficulties of Father Braun's interpretation is transferring the accent from Jesus to Mary; in fact, according to this interpretation, the hour in question is the hour when Mary can legitimately intervene in the work of salvation. Objection has been raised that in this case the text should have read, "Your hour has not come."[44] But Jesus actually said, "My hour," and his own manifestation is concerned throughout the whole episode. Furthermore, once Christ speaks to the servants in the performance of the miracle, Mary withdraws, and the narrative does not mention her again.

This central place of Christ is made more clear by the fact that Mary's action derives all its merit not from her right as mother but from her faith in the Son of God. The power that Mary has in her collaboration lies in this faith alone and, consequently, rests on Christ and recognizes in him the absolute primacy which is part of his divinity.

The incident of Cana, likewise, brings us precious indications of the *relationship between Mary and the Church*. The first lesson that stands out in this regard consists *in the initiating role which Mary's faith played in regard to the faith of the disciples*. Mary's faith brings forth the miracle and the miracle leads to a result, the importance of which is expressly emphasized by the Evangelist when he ends the narrative with these words,". . . . . and his disciples believed in him." Thus is revealed the primacy of Mary's faith, which is at the origin of the faith of the Church.

Up to this moment, we might say it was Mary in whom faith in Christ had been concentrated and hidden; it was Mary who closeted and built up in her heart the treasures of faith of the Church to come. During the long years at Nazareth, the discovery of the divine person of Jesus had been gradually developed in the light of the message of the Annunciation and from other events which since then had supernaturally enlightened his destiny. Here at the wedding feast of Cana, this faith manifests its greatness and begins to communicate itself to others.

We must particularly remark the progress of Mary's faith since the episode of the loss of the Child in the Temple. At that time, she had not understood Jesus' answer, "Did you not know that I must be about my Father's business?" (Luke 2:49). Since then, she had fathomed this word which she had kept in her heart and had learned to discern in Jesus more and more clearly the Son of the heavenly Father. We have noted that her attitude at Cana proves that she speaks to Jesus as to the Son of God, who is empowered to advance an hour fixed by the divine will. It is this faith that gives her assurance in her petition.

Consequently, at the opening of the public life, Mary is in possession of the faith that Saint John will desire for the readers of his Gospel: "These (miracles) are written that you may believe that Jesus is the Christ, the Son of God, and that believing you may have life in his name" (John 20:33). That faith which she possesses in any miracle, Mary really desires to transmit to others through the miracle performed by Jesus. Her influence on the faith of the disciples was in a way intentional; by her request Mary, in fact, desired to make known to others the divine power and goodness of Christ. By her own will, she therefore collaborated in the germination of the faith of the Church.

On the other hand, this influence of Mary did not claim

to accomplish anything except through Christ himself. It operated by the intermediary of the miracle. We repeat here what we have said concerning the absolute priority of Christ in the action and role of Mary; it is Christ who constitutes the center, and through him that role is efficacious. Mary's faith precedes and leads to that of the Church, but by virtue of Christ on whom it is founded.

In regard to the servants, the Blessed Virgin's influence is also exercised in a certain measure in the spirit of faith, at least in the sense of showing confidence in the power of Christ, by executing his orders whatever they may be. But its essence is *obedience*. Her order, "Do whatever he says," recommends complete submission founded on a confidence that accepts even the lack of understanding. And we must point out how completely the order was fulfilled. The Gospel expressly retained this significant detail that the servants filled the water pots to the brim so as to conform perfectly to the orders that had been given them. The abundance of miraculous wine was that much greater. Mary had, therefore, fully attained her objective of assuring complete obedience to her son.

This appeal for obedience also confirms the central place that Mary's intercession wants to reserve for Christ. The direction she gives to the servants is the only note of authority that she shows, and this authority is intended solely to secure their submission to Jesus. The authority that the Church recognizes in Mary is not on a level with that of Christ nor does it curtail in any way his authority because its function is obedience to the Savior.

Finally, if we consider Mary's action not in relation to the disciples or the servants, but with the guests and the wedding couple, we note another fundamental feature of this action. When the Blessed Virgin intercedes in favor of the wedding couple to supply for the lack of wine, she is assuming a task of a motherly nature: the miracle is really the fruit of her affection, full of pity and maternal solicitude. Note that when Jesus calls her "Woman" and not "Mother" he desires to abstract from his own family ties with her, but not at all from that maternal vigilance that she shows in regard to others. Mary is not justified in expecting to obtain the miracle merely as mother of Jesus, but the maternal function that she accepts regarding men gives her a right to intercede for them that contributes to the success of her undertaking.

Besides, if we examine the scope of this motherly concern of Mary toward the wedding couple and the guests, we must agree that it is singularly in accord with the title of "Woman" in the meaning in which Christ uses the term. From the beginning of his public life, Mary has no further need to exercise her maternal solicitude for Jesus, and the renunciation of that solicitude broadens her affection by extending it to other persons. We already glimpse a truth to be more vividly manifested at Calvary: separated from her son, Mary becomes the mother of men. The public life, by placing her as "Woman" above her own personal title as mother of Jesus, extends her maternal zeal to a much wider circle.

In granting the prayer of Cana, Christ confirms this extended maternal mission and assures it a marvelous fecundity. Thus, he announces the maternal mission that Mary will assume in the Church.

Such are the characteristics of the relationship between Mary and the Church as they are prefigured in what takes place at Cana through her relationship with the disciples, the servants, and the wedding couple and guests. *The object of Mary's influence appears to be a communication of faith and obedience to Christ,* that is to say, to the fundamental Christian attitude, because this consists in believing in Christ and fulfilling his will. *The nature of that influence is established as that of a maternal function in regard to men.* If we synthesize these traits, we recognize the image of a mother of men and Christians, the one responsible for developing the life of faith and submission to Christ in men, while proving her solicitude by favors of a material or temporal order. The most striking effect of the episode is the role that is bestowed on Mary as mother of the faith of the Church.

THE MEANING OF THE EPISODE WITHIN THE GENERAL FRAMEWORK OF THE GOSPEL

In the course of an exegetic analysis of the various parts of the text, we have already alluded to connections with the rest of the Gospel. Now we should like to consider the place of the episode in the development of the gospel events viewed as a whole.

According to Saint John, the miracle of Cana is the beginning of a manifestation of the glory of Christ. Now in the entire Gospel, we must distinguish *three stages of this manifestation of Christ's glory.* First is the Incarnation itself. The Evangelist in fact, unlike Saint Paul, does not look upon it as an abasement or an annihilation in a "condition of servant," but essentially as a manifestation of glory: "And the Word was made flesh and dwelt among us.

And we saw his glory — glory as of the only begotten of the Father — full of grace and truth" (John 1:14). The second stage is Cana, the first miracle by which Christ "manifested his glory" (John 2:2). This state continues during the whole public life, where miracles follow one another but it is already dominated by the prospect of a third manifestation of glory, a supreme and final one, which will eventuate at the time of the Passion, when the Son of man "will be lifted up." This "lifting up," is the expression of both the suffering of Jesus on the cross and his final glorification.

Now Mary plays a role in each of these stages. In the first, the Incarnation, she is not named nor does she appear in Saint John's Gospel. Her intercession, nevertheless, is implied in the words of the Prologue, according to the reading of the text which appears the most probable: "Who was born not of blood, nor of the will of the flesh, nor of the will of man, but of God" (John 1:13).[45] In these words a strong insistence of the divine, not human, origin of the birth, moreover, contributes to show that it concerns Christ rather than Christians because, if it concerned Christians, there would have been no use in piling up three expressions: "not of blood, nor of the will of the flesh, nor of the will of men." Now such insistence shows at the same time how intent the mind of the author was on the role of Mary, the instrument of the virginal birth. This role is so much the more fundamental as it issues directly into the manifestation of the glory of the Word. In fact, immediately after writing "who was born not of blood . . . . . but of God," Saint John declares that the Word was made flesh and dwelt among us, that we have seen his glory; and he makes it very explicit that this glory is "as of the only-begotten of the Father." Precisely by her virginity, Mary proves her son to be born of God. By testifying that Jesus was not born of blood, nor of the will of the flesh nor of the will of man, the virginal maternity brings to light the divine filiation of Christ. It contributes to the manifestation of the glory of Christ "as of the only-begotten Son of the Father." There is scarcely need to emphasize the eminence of this role of the Virgin, as collaborator with the Father, in giving birth to the Incarnate Word.

Therefore, since Mary held this essential role in the origin of the first manifestation of glory at the moment of the Incarnation, it is easier to understand the role with which she was endowed at the wedding feast of Cana, in originating the second stage of the manifestation of glory, that of the public life and the miracles. The two functions are the extensions of each other. Here again, Mary is the collaborator with the Father in a unique right: she is called to concur with him in determining the hour and the circumstances in which the glory of the Savior will be revealed to men. The first miracle in some sort is virginally brought forth by Mary, in such a way that, like Jesus himself in his human nature, it appears as the fruit of the Father and of Mary indissolubly united in their action.

Finally, Mary's presence will be expressly noted again by Saint John at the third manifestation of glory, which completes the first two. We shall have occasion later to determine the meaning of this presence. Let us simply remark that it implies a part in the glorification of Christ, not only in his sufferings and his sacrifice since, according to the words of Jesus related by the Evangelist, the cross itself is already a lifting up in glory.

The Mystery of Cana

From this point of view, it is important to note the parallelism between the scene at Cana and at Calvary. While admitting that the expression "my hour" relates exclusively to the first miracle, it must be recognized that the hour of the first revelation of the Messiah was oriented toward the decisive hour of the supreme glorification of Christ, and consequently, the role assumed by Mary at the wedding of Cana prepared the role which she was to assume at the prime moment of the redemption. This connection the studies of Father Gaechter and Father Braun have had the distinction of emphasizing.

This perspective of orientation toward the hour of Calvary helps us to understand why Mary's intercession at Cana is the only intervention allowed to her in the public life of Jesus. Because such intercession is *of the order of a sign,* a sign does not need to be multiplied. It is enough for it to be made once, and its part has been played. The miracles of the public life are precisely in the order of sign and are, moreover, called "signs" by Saint John. They have been performed for the purpose of signifying, of revealing symbolically the Messianic power of Christ. These material favors indicate his spiritual power to renew souls. The cures of the blind, paralytic, and lepers are intended to show that it is Christ who brings remedy to moral infirmities, spreads light, breaks the chains of sin and purifies consciences. The miracle of Cana symbolizes Christ's power to relieve human deficiencies and to transform the things of this world; soon we shall speak of its symbolic significance. In fact, all these acts are previous manifestations of the power to save, which Christ will actually be able to exercise fully at the moment of his glorification after he shall have merited salvation for men by his death. The period of the public life therefore has a provisional character, giving a foretaste by signs of what will become an accomplished fact on Calvary.

For this reason Mary's action at Cana also assumes a provisional character with the force of a sign. It is intended to show what her intercession will be in the exercise that the glorified Christ will make of his redeeming power, and to emphasize the role played by Mary in putting this power into action. That sign did not need to be reproduced elsewhere. It was given at Cana in a sufficient and very eloquent manner: Mary calls forth the first miracle which will unlatch all the others so that the whole series is dependent on the intercession of Mary. The primacy of the Virgin's action signifies the importance of her mediation in the whole course of the work of salvation.

THE MEANING OF THE EPISODE CONSIDERED IN THE DIVINE PLAN

The miracle of Cana was performed at the request of Mary, who succeeded in obtaining the advancement of the hour of the first public revelation of the Savior. But this initiatory role of Mary does not by any means nullify the fact that the whole episode was according to the divine plan. The place of the event in the general framework of the Gospel would be enough to show that it formed part of that plan of God. In fact Mary's intervention at the opening of the public life is integrated in the more general role of Mary in the work of salvation and in the manifestation of Christ's glory. It is in accord with the mission that she filled in the Incarnation and with that which will devolve upon her at Calvary. If the will of the Father determined that role for the Incarnation and Calvary, it likewise did so for Cana.

Besides, when we say that by her prayer Mary obtained a change of the hour and of the circumstances of the first miracle, we must add that that prayer had been motivated by divine inspiration. It is true that God changed the hour at the request of Mary and that, if Mary had not of her own accord intervened or had not persevered in her confident assurance, the first miracle would not have taken place at Cana. But this change of hour had itself been foreseen and willed by God, who decided beforehand to promote Mary's prayer and to hear it.

Since the episode is part of the divine plan and, moreover, holds a place of distinction in it, we are fully authorized in taking a much wider meaning from it by comparing it with other parts of that plan. It is not at all necessary that the Evangelist should have wanted to suggest that meaning to us, nor even that he should have noticed it. In fact, such meaning is based not only on the text, but on the connection between the episode and other events: it is simply necessary that this connection be so striking as to impose the idea of divine intention.

Such will be the basis of the symbolic meanings that men will seek to establish for the miracle. There is no symbolic meaning clearly suggested by the evangelist. But that is no reason for excluding them as arbitrary or as an abstraction. Even if Saint John did not wish to tell us that there was a symbol of the Eucharist in the miracle, we ourselves shall recognize this symbol if we notice a relationship between the nature of the miracle and the sacrament instituted at the

Cenacle. The symbolic meaning will rely upon the unity of the divine plan which arranged the whole episode of Cana as part of the more extensive work of salvation.

We pointed out that at first glance the wedding feast of Cana did not appear as a favorable setting for the first manifestation of the glory of the Savior, and that we could have thought of a first miracle which would give a more substantial setting than wine for a feast. Now the analysis of the miracle shows how admirably the setting was utilized by the divine plan so that the event is presented with a wealth of meaning and in remarkable concordance with the general effect of the work of Christ. The divine intention which has directed everything is already revealed in the way by which the narrative itself expresses Mary's role because that is the role that the Church today attributes to Mary. Later, the divine intention will be still more evident by comparison with other aspects of the plan of salvation.

1. The Role of Mary and the Role of Eve

It would be too much to pretend that the name "Woman" addressed to Mary by Jesus, is an allusion to the person of Eve. Nevertheless, we have noted that it could not be an ordinary title like that which Christ addressed to other women because the appropriate name for her would have been "Mother." The title "Woman" indicated that Jesus wished to raise his mother to a higher level, that of the Messianic work, which was not regulated by familial relationship. We added that this name was most meaningful if we remembered that in his public life Jesus called himself, the "Son of man," in order to designate himself in his official mission, Messiah, both human and divine. The title "Woman" forms a contrast, in a way, with that of "Son of man" to indicate the position that Mary holds in regard to the Messiah.

Now this position recalls that of Eve in respect to Adam. The relationship is evident from the fact that in the divine plan the redemption is in answer to the fall. Christ is the new Adam, Mary is the new Eve (I Cor. 15:45). In the drama of Eden, the actors had been a man and a woman. At Cana, at the beginning of the ministry which will lead to redemption, the actors are the Son of man and the woman. There is then an analogy with this one difference: formerly, the woman was the spouse while now she is the mother; in both cases, however, the woman is the partner with the man or with the Son of man.

At Cana as in the garden of Eden, there is *a manifestation of glory desired by the woman*. It is the woman who plays the initiating role and who leads man in the way in which she wishes to lead him.

In this analogy, there are glaring differences. At the suggestion of the devil, Eve coveted divine glory: "You shall be as gods" (Gen. 3:5). Pride and selfishness moved the woman to seek to plunder that glory of equality with God. In Mary's case, on the contrary, it was not selfishness but altruism because she does not desire glory for herself; she desires the manifestation of the glory of her son and she desires it through love for men who are to benefit by it. There is no attempt at plunder,[46] no desire to appropriate something unjustly, for Mary asks this manifestation because she believes in the divinity of her son and considers that divine glory is legitimately his. Furthermore, she is acting under divine inspiration according to the lights which have come to her from above since the day of the Annunciation. No pride or personal ambition exists in her, nor any desire for independence or liberty like that which had motivated Eve. At Cana, Mary makes her request with profound respect for the authority of Christ and the will of the Father. Her directions to the servants show that she submits herself entirely to the decision of Jesus, whatever it may be, and that she encourages others to the same submission. With the unwavering initiative of her action, she succeeds in getting complete docility to the divine plan. She obtains the manifestation of Christ's glory by an attitude similar to that by which Christ will obtain his final glorification, obedience. This is her answer to the disobedience of Eve.

2. The Banquet of the Messianic Nuptials

We cannot fail to be stirred by the fact that the setting of the first miracle fulfills two fundamental figures which served to express the Messianic period and which Christ used on other occasions to teach that this time has come: the symbol of the banquet and the symbol of the nuptials.

Under the form of a feast God had promised salvation to his people and to all peoples, a feast at which there would be no mourning, no death, no tears, and no shame. Later, Jesus will announce that "the kingdom of heaven is to be compared to a king who made a marriage feast for his son" (Matt. 22:2-14). In this way he unites the image of the banquet with that of the wedding; in another place he presents himself as the spouse who rejoices the children of the wedding, that is to say the disciples, and who bids the wise virgins enter with him into the marriage hall.[47] (Matt. 9:15; Mark 2:19; Luke 5:34; Matt. 25:1-12). Returning again to a comparison of the wedding that the Old Testament had used, he applies it to himself to show the ideal union of *Yahweh* with the elect nation.[48] The two figures are intended to call forth the joy that God offers to men through the Messiah; the joy of the feast by a surfeit of all good things and the joy of the nuptials through the love of God who comes to men and rouses in them a reciprocal love.

In their simplicity, the nuptials of Cana represent the picture of Messianic joy in a concrete manner. By the miracle performed there that constitutes the first revelation of the Messiah, the wedding feast is symbolically raised to the rank of a Messianic banquet where Christ is the central figure: he gives the wine. Wine was of primary importance in a banquet as is proved by the simple fact that "feast" in Hebrew means "the act of drinking." By this same fact, Jesus appears as the true spouse, the provider of the feast.

Consequently, the miracle of Cana proves that the union between God and men, predicted for the time of the Messiah, is beginning to be realized, *that the divine spouse is giving himself to mankind*. The setting of the wedding feast is a manifestation that the first revelation of the glory of the Messiah is the result of a demonstration not only of power but of love, and that Christ's intention is to bind himself to men. This manifestation of love is so much the more engaging because it demonstrates a bounty in Christ which, far from placing an accent on austerity, desires to pour itself out in even material benefits. God appears as a true spouse, full of affection and benevolence, and inaugurates the reign of complete love and definitive union.

Furthermore, the feast provided by Christ symbolizes *the joy* which is to be poured out upon men, the joy of the presence of the spouse. This joy accompanies an *extraordinary abundance of good things*. The Evangelist insisted on telling of the capacity of the urns which Jesus ordered to be filled, so that we could judge the quantity of wine furnished by the miracle. It is a considerable quantity, far beyond the needs of the wedding. Christ wanted to indicate the generosity with which spiritual blessings would be granted to men. Here we recognize the lavish abundance promised for the Messianic epoch. By having the urns filled, Christ showed his desire to fill hearts with joy, according to the expressions which he will use later: "These things I have spoken to you that my joy may be in you, and that your joy may be made full" (John 15:11); "That they may have my joy made full in themselves" (John 17:13); "That your joy be full" (John 16:24).

The details of the miracle make very clear the lavishness with which divine blessings are henceforth to be bestowed. The narrative mentions the purpose of the urns; they were not earthen urns for ordinary household use but stone urns set out for the legal ablutions. That is why many exegetes have recognized in the episode a figure of *the substitution of the new economy of salvation for the old economy of legal observance.*[49] The urns which had permitted the accomplishment of the Law are raised to a higher purpose: to give wine for the Messianic banquet. It is a radical transformation but it is important to observe how Christ proceeds to it. He takes the Law itself as a point of departure and in its development he works a revolution. He begins by having the urns filled, and this act seems a material image concretizing his declaration: "I have not come to destroy (the Law) but to fulfill" (Matt. 5:17). In fulfilling or accomplishing the Law he goes beyond and transforms it.

Some of Jesus' disciples must have been struck by that transformation; those who formerly were disciples of John the Baptist were formed to a severe asceticism that tended to reinforce legal prescriptions. Christ's action in giving an abundance of wine at the wedding must have been a revelation to them, not only of the omnipotence of the Master, but also of the atmosphere and the orientation of his message, authentic deliverance from the narrowness of a depressing asceticism and from a Law which stifled the spirit. Therefore, Father Lagrange thinks that since the disciples were witnesses of the miracle, they probably had a certain intuition of the new order that Christ was going to found.[50]

On the other hand, it is highly significant that the transformation of water into wine involves *a creation*. The miracle of Cana is a miracle operated by a Creator. From this point of view, it is a clearer proof of the power of Christ than the healing miracles in which Jesus appears as one who sets aside the obstacle of infirmity or breaks the chains of malady. Here something new, the wine, surges up by the power of Christ and testifies to the divine nature of this power since only God can create. It is the announcement that the reign of salvation will bring a new creation and that Christ will not confine himself to curing or to transforming men, but will remake them by giving them a higher nature.

If we determine the symbolic meaning of this miracle as the installation of the Messianic kingdom, at the same time, we discover the extent of Mary's role. Since she instigated the miracle, she is symbolically presented to us *as she who introduces into this world the union or nuptials of God and man, the abundance of Messianic goods, the plenitude of the joy of Christ in hearts, the transformation of the kingdom of the Law into the reign of true salvation, the new creation of the universe and of men.* Of course, she does none of this by herself: at Cana, her intervention consists simply in being the cause of her son's acting. Her mission could be defined as that of introducing Christ to the wedding. Probably because of her, Jesus had been invited with his disciples to take part in the feast; certainly at her instance he sets out to play the role of spouse by giving the miraculous wine. Through Mary, therefore, divine love and divine life enter into an earthly and human setting. Notice that she does not concur physically in the performance of the miracle nor participate in the actual action of Christ. She has merely triggered that action *by a moral influence, intercession.*

Must we add that this role of introducing the divine spouse into this world corresponds in a striking manner with the role that Mary played at the time of the Incarnation? Then she had introduced on earth the person of the Messiah; now she introduces among men the transforming and recreating action of Christ.

Finally, the image of the Messianic nuptial banquet draws our attention back to Calvary. It is in the passion that the love which Christ brings to men as bridegroom will be consummated; by designating himself thus, he will not fail to announce the day when the bridegroom will be taken away from his disciples (Matt. 9:15; Mark 2:20; Luke 5:35). We know that Saint Paul will see in the sacrifice of the cross the model of conjugal love, the consummation of the marriage of Christ with his Church (Ephes. 5:25). The Messianic feast will be envisaged by him also as a consequence and further effect of his death: "But I say to you, I will not drink henceforth of this fruit of the vine, until that day when I shall drink it new with you in the kingdom of my Father" (Matt. 26:29). The wine of Cana was already given in the light of this; and the stone urns, intended for the legal purifications, had been filled with a view to a final purification which the work of redemption would operate.

According to the divine plan, therefore, *the mission attributed to Mary at the wedding of Cana needed to be completed by a mission in juxtaposition with the act of Christ which would consummate the nuptials and merit the installation of the heavenly feast.*

3. The Sacramental Economy

Since, in the divine plan, the incident of Cana manifests the engagement of Christ in the new order of salvation, it will not be surprising that the symbolism at the same time concerns certain aspects essential to the sacramental life of the Church. In fact, the sacraments apply the merits of salvation through efficacious signs. A miracle is very specially apt to suggest the sacrament since it is in the order of a sign.[51]

[171]

Mary in the Gospel

a. THE EUCHARIST

The first sacrament which the episode of Cana brings to the mind of the reader is the Eucharist. We do not possess any certain indication that the Evangelist thought of this Eucharistic symbolism or wished to express it in his narrative. But the structure of the miracle as well as a parallelism with the miracle of the multiplication of the loaves seems to show clearly that Christ had the Eucharist in view at Cana.

Father Gaechter draws attention to the fact that, like the multiplication of the loaves, the miracle of Cana took place *near the Jewish Passover*[52] (John 2:13; 6:4). This nearness seems to indicate that Christ's intention in performing the miracle was related to the true Paschal repast, the Eucharistic Supper. That date of the miracle is more impressive still, if we consider the succession of the three feasts of the Passover mentioned in the public life of Christ: before the first, the wine is given at Cana; before the second, the bread is multiplied for the crowds; on the eve of the last, the bread and wine are consecrated into the body and blood of the Lord. These three feasts of Passover are therefore aligned in a Eucharistic perspective opened up by the miracle of Cana.

Furthermore, it is important to note that the first miracle, by its structure, can symbolize the Eucharist better than the later miracle of the multiplication of the loaves. It is produced as a transformation of water into wine, *a transformation which suggests the Eucharistic transsubstantiation.* On the other hand, the multiplication of the loaves does not involve a similar transformation, and if Christ explicitly

[172]

presented this miracle as the announcement of the Eucharist, with much greater reason must we recognize that symbolism at Cana.

This significance of the miracle of Cana is a harmonious complement to the preparation for the Eucharist. Not only bread, but also wine, are subjects of a preparatory miracle. Thus, the two elements of the consecration have been prefigured in a miraculous action performed by Christ. The Eucharistic discourse which Jesus will hold after the multiplication of the loaves will really be based on the two miracles which justify more fully the declaration: "He who eats my flesh and drinks my blood has life everlasting" (John 6:55).

Finally, the symbolism of the Eucharist results from the close connection that exists between the Messianic banquet and the Eucharistic banquet. At the Last Supper, on the occasion of the institution of the Eucharist, Christ alluded to the Messianic banquet of which he was going to taste after his sacrifice (Matt. 26:29; Mark 14:25). Cana suggests the Messianic banquet but, at the same time, it also presents the image of the Eucharistic banquet. The Eucharist is precisely the sacrament which is the sign of the Messianic feast.

This Eucharistic symbolism leads us to consider the problem of Mary's role in the gift of the Eucharist. The problem does not arise from the literal meaning of the narrative since the Eucharistic symbolism is not demonstrated through that literal sense. It is in the light of the divine plan as it appeared in later theological reflection that we can raise the question and give a legitimate extension to the sparse indications of the text. The role that Mary plays in setting up the

Messianic banquet entails a role in the gift of the Eucharist since this is the earthly realization of that banquet. In the episode of the wedding at Cana, we are struck by the initiative taken by Mary, especially if we compare it with the conduct of the disciples at the multiplication of the loaves. The sight of a hungry crowd, far from urging the disciples to ask Christ for miraculous nourishment, impelled them to advise sending everyone away. This conduct is diametrically opposed to that of Mary. She, on the contrary, wants to avoid sending away the wedding guests and asks that wine be given miraculously. Obviously, she does not ask for this wine as a symbol of the Eucharist since she does not yet know anything about that sacrament. Her request asks for and obtains a certain gift from Christ to man in the form of wine. If later facts from Revelation make us think that Christ attached a Eucharistic symbolism to the miracle, they permit us to add that it seemed by that very fact to extend the initiating role of Mary to the Eucharist, at least under the form of an aspiration for the most complete gift of the Savior to men.

The comparison with the multiplication of the loaves points out another difference between Mary and the apostles. Mary remains apart from the actual accomplishment of the miracle and does not play any role in the distribution of the miraculous wine. The disciples, on the contrary, are the agents that Christ uses to distribute the miraculous bread among the crowd; to their own stupefaction, their role is announced to them at the beginning by the words of the Master: "You yourselves give them some food" (Matt. 14:16; Mark 6:37; Luke 9:13). This role prefigures that of their priesthood in which they will be the instruments of

Christ in the making and distribution of the Eucharistic bread. Mary, on her part, is not destined to the priesthood; at Cana, she does not serve as instrument in the action of Christ. We must repeat what we have said in regard to her mission in the Messianic banquet and the reign of salvation. *It is a mission not of physical concurrence but of intercession and moral influence. It is a mission of introducing: Mary introduces the Eucharistic Christ to mankind.*

This mission of introducing, likewise, explains the fact that Mary is present at Cana, whereas she intervenes neither in the multiplication of the loaves nor in the Last Supper. The miracle of Cana opens up the Eucharistic perspective. Once Christ has entered along this path, Mary has nothing to do but withdraw for she has done her part. She is not invested with the mission of a priest and can, therefore, be absent from the multiplication of the loaves and the Last Supper, but she is not thereby prevented from playing a highly significant part, according to the symbolism of Cana, in the introduction of the mystery of the Eucharist.

Nevertheless, what is still wanting to her mission regarding the Eucharist is the role that she is to assume on Calvary since the Eucharist depends on the final sacrifice of Christ. At the foot of the cross, *Mary will experience the full burden* of pain of the Eucharistic gift of Christ. At Cana she had wished only one thing, the greatest gift of the Messiah to men in the wine that he would furnish them miraculously. On Golgotha, she will be asked to accept all the consequences of that gift in order that the figure of Cana may become a reality. Thus, in her role of initiator to which she had already given the full measure of her faith, Mary must make the complete offering of herself and, at the price of excruciating suffering, give Christ up definitively for the Eucharistic repast of mankind.

b. The Marriage

The banquet of the Messianic nuptials results from the fusion of two images: banquet and nuptials. The sacrament which corresponds to the banquet is the Eucharist. Now we must consider the sacrament which corresponds to the nuptials.

It is very evident that Christ's presence at the wedding of Cana was intended to consecrate matrimony. In Saint John, the narrative of the episode immediately follows that of the vocation of the disciples. Now in calling his disciples, Jesus took them away from their family connections and proposed to them the ideal of renouncing marriage so as to occupy themselves solely with the kingdom of heaven (Matt. 19:12). This ideal of celibacy for religious reasons was that of John the Baptist. Christ himself adopted it. We might have thought that Christ was not interested in marriage and did not desire to consider it of any particular religious merit. Everything tends to make us think that Christ desired to react against this impression. Immediately after he has called his disciples and has urged them to a higher life, he goes to a wedding. Thus he testifies publicly to his approbation of the married way of life. We have the impression that, after having established celibacy for those who are specially called to follow him, he wishes to consecrate by his presence the more common state of marriage.

Furthermore, the miracle which he performs shows his intention to transform marriage by providing it with his own wine, far superior to the ordinary wine that nature furnishes. It is a symbol of his love which he wishes to make the center and basis of conjugal union. He establishes marriage on a supernatural level where conjugal love is to draw its substance from divine love. Thus, Saint Paul will say of marriage that that mystery is great in relation to Christ and the Church (Ephes. 5:32); the love of the spouses is founded on that of Christ who has loved the Church to the point of delivering himself for her in sacrifice. Symbolically, at Cana, Christ acts as the bridegroom who gives to the marriage the wine which will assure its permanence.

Now Mary was specially chosen to play a role in that prefiguration of the consecration of marriage. Indeed, although she had perfectly fulfilled the ideal of virginity, she had been engaged by the divine will in the bonds of matrimony. Evidently God arranged the episode of Cana with the symbolism of the sanctification of marriage to mark Mary's role in that sanctification. According to a divine plan whose ultimate purpose is yet unknown to her, when Mary saves the wedding from a miserable, disastrous end, she is fulfilling her mission *of safeguarding marriage from human deficiencies and of introducing into it the regenerating love of Christ.*

This is the prefiguration of Mary's intervention in the sacramental economy. Since the Blessed Virgin is invested with a general mission in the whole economy of salvation, her influence extends to all sacramental graces. The mystery of Cana more clearly indicates by its symbolism the relationship between Mary and two sacraments because in these two cases, there is a special affinity. The gift of the Eucharist is akin to the maternal solicitude of Mary for men; the duty of a mother is to provide for the nourishment of her children. The consecration of marriage is in accord with a deep aspiration that Mary must have had since she, who had found eminent sanctity in that state and had been witness of many conjugal afflictions, sought divine help to sustain and transform the married state.

IV

The Mystery of Calvary

I. Analysis and Theological Value of the Narrative

MARY'S PRESENCE BY THE CROSS

"Now there were standing by the cross of Jesus his mother and his mother's sister, Mary of Cleophas, and Mary Magdalen" (John 19:25). When we read this sentence of Saint John and compare it with what Saint Mark and Saint Matthew tell us about the presence of many women near the Crucified, we are astonished that these Evangelists did not mention the mother of Christ among these women. They cite, however, other names: Mary Magdalen, Mary the mother of James and Joseph, and Salome the mother of James and John (Matt. 27:55; Mark 15:40). These are the names of women who followed Jesus and served him; thus we have confirmation that Mary did not form part of the group of women who accompanied Jesus during the public life and gave him aid in goods or services. Saint Luke did not mention the mother of the Savior among them (Luke 8:2-3). This customary retirement of Mary gives greater importance to her presence on Calvary.

Saint John is the only Evangelist to grasp this importance. Although to the other narrators of the Passion, Mary seems anonymously lost among the great number of women who are not far from the cross, John draws our attention to her. He does so because Christ himself, at this moment, wanted to distinguish his mother from all of those other women who were present. To her alone Christ spoke individually from the height of the cross. Therefore, it is the Savior who makes us discover something exceptional, something unique, in this presence so like the others exteriorly. The words of the Master from the cross reveal to us the meaning of Mary's presence according to the divine plan.

Regarding the Blessed Virgin's interior dispositions, the mention of her presence on Calvary leads us to suppose that *she was there of her own accord*. Mary is there because she wants to be there. Very likely the women with whom she had come to Jerusalem, particularly her cousin, Mary the wife of Cleophas, had made some effort to spare her the sight of the suffering of Jesus, as any one might do through pity for a mother in such circumstances; but every attempt to turn her from the way to Golgotha had been thwarted by her firm determination to follow Christ to the end. Even more, this intention to associate herself with the tragic fate of Jesus must have been the reason for her setting out from Galilee to go to Jerusalem. In fact, Mary knew the threat of death which hung over her son. When the Master had returned to Judea to raise Lazarus from the dead, the disciples had objected that the Jews were seeking to stone him and at the time of the departure, Thomas had said, "Let us also go that we may die with him" (John 11:16). If the apostles had such fears, we must presume that Mary shared them and went to Jerusalem because she particularly wanted to be near Jesus at the moment of danger. Would she not have been more ready than anyone else to "die with him?" Therefore, she had come to the Holy City filled with foreboding, but resolved to have an integral part in the fate of her son.

With good reason, then, we must conclude that Mary's presence by the cross was not the mere result of a combination of circumstances, but proceeded from the firm determination of Mary to be united with the dramatic destiny of Christ.

"WOMAN, BEHOLD THY SON."

1. Messianic Value of the Declaration

Although many exegetes have interpreted this word as an expression of filial solicitude on the part of Christ who wanted to provide for the future of his mother, Father Gaechter has correctly insisted on the insufficiency of such an interpretation and shown that the words of the Savior in union with the whole setting have a Messianic significance.[1] It is not a matter of an action concerning the personal situation of Mary alone and of the beloved disciple, but *a symbol which forms part of the work of redemption* and consequently has a much wider meaning. These reasons form the basis for this broader interpretation.

(1.) The time would not have been suitable for making arrangements for the private affairs of Mary for the future. Jesus would not have waited for the moment when he was about to die, if he had wanted to provide for his mother's

[181]

future. He would have done so much earlier. This is all the more evident because provision had to be made for Mary at the beginning of the public life. When he began his apostolic ministry, Jesus once and for all gave up the companionship of his mother; furthermore, we know that Mary did not follow Jesus in his journeyings and her presence on Calvary was by way of exception. Consequently, arrangement for Mary's shelter and support must already have been made. This problem, therefore, did not remain to be settled; simply from the point of view of providing for Mary, the means adopted during the public life could continue after the death of Christ.

(2.) The details that the Gospel gives us concerning the scene on Calvary show us that no intervention by Jesus was called for either because of the needs of Mary or of his beloved disciple. At the time, Mary was with her "sister" or relative, Mary, the cousin of Cleophas, who was certainly ready to procure for her all she would need. If the action of Christ was interpreted as an effort to procure protection and shelter for his mother, it would have seemed pointless, even somewhat offensive, to the "sister" of Mary, since it would have implied that she was unable or unwilling to fulfill the duty to help one another which falls on close relatives. On the other hand, neither did John have any need of a mother; his mother was standing nearby. If it had been a question of setting up a family relationship, the solution adopted by Jesus would have postulated a need which did not exist and it would have been insulting to the wife of Zebedee to be deprived of her own function as mother. Finally, let us note that Christ, who required his disciples to give up their families, had included his beloved disciple in this sacrifice and, therefore, would not have intended to give John a mother on a private familial basis because the Master had already asked him to give up his own.

(3.) More explicitly, the whole trend of the episode indicates an official act of worldwide importance. Is it not the peak of the public life of Christ, that solemn hour toward which his whole ministry on earth was oriented? It is really the supreme hour when the Savior consummates his mission of redemption, and we would find it difficult to understand that he would have chosen this moment for an insertion of private and family preoccupation. His action, therefore, can be interpreted only in connection with the accomplishment of his public mission. Besides, the very text of the Gospel is at pains to confirm what was sufficiently apparent in the rest of the context. Immediately after relating this episode, Saint John writes: "After this, Jesus, knowing that all things were now accomplished . . ." (John 19:28). Thus, the Evangelist explicitly mentions that in the mind of Jesus the declaration made to Mary and to the beloved disciple put the finishing touch on what he was to accomplish, the mission entrusted by his Father.

(4.) The title, "Woman," also shows that Christ had risen above familial relations with his mother. If, at that moment, he had wanted to show his affection to her by an act of filial devotion, he would spontaneously have addressed her as "Mother." When we made an analysis of the narrative of Cana, we noted all that Christ meant in using the title of "Woman." We showed clearly his intention of disregarding the status of the hidden life and of looking on

Mary only with respect to her intervention in the accomplishment of the Messianic function. On Calvary this name keeps its full strength in order to exclude any sign of filial intimacy and resolutely to place the relations of the crucified with Mary on a higher plane, that of his work for mankind.

(5.) No less revealing is the fact that Christ begins by entrusting the beloved disciple to Mary. A sign of filial solicitude would normally have required that Christ entrust his mother to the disciple first, or even solely, so that the latter could take care of her, surround her with affection, and protect her. By speaking to Mary first with the words, "Behold thy son," Christ shows his desire that, contrary to what might have been expected, Mary should take care of the disciple. Such care could evidently not be made on an individual level: it was a mission vested in the Blessed Virgin, a mission closely related to the work of redemption which the Lord was in the act of consummating.

Every indication of text and context, therefore, invites us to recognize in Christ's declaration not an act of filial solicitude but of his public mission as Savior.

The Evangelist, who expressly related to us these words of Christ at the supreme moment of the accomplishment of the work of redemption, by adding that after that Jesus was aware that all things had been accomplished, seems to have clearly recognized the official, Messianic value of the declaration. In what, precisely, did that value consist for him? The text does not give us any information in that regard, and the author, perhaps, did not have a clear idea of it. In order to determine the meaning that the Savior attached to his words, since his intention extended beyond what even the Evangelist himself could understand and express, all we can do is study the suggestions and details furnished by the declaration itself, in the setting in which it was pronounced. Let us try to determine the nature, the extent, and the basis of the motherhood granted to Mary.

2. Nature of the Motherhood

Regarding the nature of that motherhood, it is immediately apparent that Christ did not intend merely to establish between Mary and the beloved disciple the relationship of mother-and-son *affection*. The episode is not to be understood as a scene of endearment in which Jesus, moved by pity for his mother and for his disciple at the moment he is leaving them, desires to satisfy the demands of their love and bind them in a reciprocal attachment. Certainly, the words, "Behold thy son," imply the birth of a new affection in Mary toward the beloved disciple, just as the words, "Behold thy mother," will draw the disciple to a filial love toward Mary. But this consideration of affection is only secondary, a consequence of a more fundamental function of Mary in the work of redemption.

Christ assigns to the Virgin a *mission* as mother in regard to the disciple, a mission which enters into the framework of the salvation granted to men. Mary's role is not terminated at the cross; it is only beginning. The Savior confides the disciple to her at the moment when he obtains from his Father through his sacrifice the salvation of mankind. He asks her to watch over this disciple as a mother: this task can consist only in promoting by maternal action the development of the spiritual life, of that new life which is going to be diffused in souls. In other words, it concerns a maternal function destined to be accomplished in the order of grace, a grace that Christ by virtue of the merits of his Passion, is going to spread among his disciples. Mary is called to play a maternal role in the diffusion of spiritual blessings that the blood and water soon to be poured out by the blow of the lance will symbolize.

But the words, "Behold thy son," express something still more fundamental than a mission. They indicate a new *state,* a new *quality* of Mary, a primordial quality on which the mission is founded. Incidental to the function of motherhood is the fact of being a mother, and it is this fact that the Savior proclaims. Jesus does not say, "Woman, treat him as if he were your son," nor "Woman, consider him as thy son," nor did he say to John: "Look upon her as thy mother." He declares in the most absolute manner: "Woman, behold thy son," "Behold thy mother." He postulates a new truth by conferring on Mary and on the disciple respectively the qualities of mother and of son. At the moment when these words are pronounced, according to the plan of the economy of redemption, Mary becomes actually the mother of the disciple. Furthermore, à propos of this declaration of Jesus, some one has spoken of "an action in a way sacramental."[2] In fact, the word operates what it signifies: it makes the disciple the real son of Mary.

Christ did not confine himself to declaring or stating an already existing reality; he actually constitutes Mary mother of the disciple. Formerly this maternity did not exist; the germ was contained in the maternity of Mary in regard to the Savior, but it was only a germ, and it needed the divine action to develop it and bring it to maturity. It is the authority of the Savior, his creative and redeeming power, which at this moment accomplishes in Mary a signal transformation and raises her to a new motherhood.

3. Extension of the Maternity

We have reached the point of emphasizing the extension of Mary's maternity according to the measure of the official Messianic declaration which the word of the Master possessed. The beloved disciple was designated son of Mary, not in his own individual right, but as a disciple. If the new motherhood of Mary is set in the order of the new life brought by Christ, it concerns John insofar as he is engaged in that life. This motherhood, then, does not regard him exclusively and is not given in recognition of his personal qualities, but it applies to that within him which constitutes him a disciple of Christ. Ontologically, this motherhood is given to every man called to be a true disciple of Christ. *On the Messianic plane* where it is proclaimed, the motherhood of Mary cannot be limited to a private relationship with John, but must have a *universal scope*.

For this reason, since Christ was acting as Savior of mankind, the beloved disciple was regarded by him as a symbol of all other disciples. It does not, however, necessarily follow that the choice of the beloved disciple for the proclamation of the universal maternity of Mary should be deprived of significance. The choice is intended to make us understand the meaning of this maternity better. First, negatively, the fact that it is not Peter, the chief of the apostles, who has been designated son of Mary, is very enlightening. Christ did not institute the motherhood of Mary as a superior degree of the hierarchy of his Church. This maternity is placed not in the hierarchical order of which Peter was the representative, but in the order of intimacy of life with Christ, or of the communication of the life of Christ. Positively, in fact, John possesses the following characteristics: he is the disciple whom Jesus specially loves, who rested on the bosom of the Master at the Last Supper and received consequently a particular privilege of intimacy with him; immediately after he has been declared the son of Mary, he is going to be the witness of the pouring out of blood and water that the blow of the lance will provoke, an outpouring which symbolizes the gifts of spiritual and sacramental life which the death of Christ is meriting for mankind. There is, then, a special bond between John and Jesus, both in the affective realm of love and in the effective communication of the blessings which accompany that love. This status of beloved disciple accentuates the meaning of Mary's motherhood; we become sons of Mary by reason of a special love which Christ bears to his disciples and in order that we may have part in the new life that his love wishes to diffuse. The characteristic traits of the beloved disciple are no motive for confining to him alone the filiation which Christ has pronounced; they form part of the symbol and have universal value. However, they merely accentuate the characteristic traits of all disciples, for all disciples are those whom Jesus loves, all have been called to share intimacy with the Master, and to all has been revealed the communication of divine life that Christ desires to give to men. John's privilege consists simply in having benefited to a higher degree from these common advantages. Here, likewise, as model and symbol he is the beneficiary of a gift which will be common to all: to be a son of Mary. He shows us that the universal motherhood of Mary is founded on a more intense love of the Savior for man, that it is bound to a life of intimacy with Christ and is ordained for the communication of the blessings of the redemption.

Does that mean, since it is a universal declaration contained in an individual symbol, that the beloved disciple must be regarded in that scene as representative of the Christian community and that Mary is proclaimed mother of the community, the Church? Father Braun proposes a communal interpretation on the passage and does not hesitate to say, with R. Bultmann, that the words addressed by Jesus to Mary have the same meaning as the words of the priestly prayer: "That they all may be one" (John 22:21). He reminds us in this regard that the unification of the faithful based on the mystery of the Incarnation is essential to the theology of Saint John. And he believes that there is evidence of this idea in the text. Since, according to the remark of Origen, Jesus in dying said to his mother, "Behold thy son," and not, "He is likewise thy son," we can legitimately conclude that in the mind of the Evangelist, the disciple is in a way identified with Jesus in whom all the disciples are united under one head.[3]

The relationship between Mary, as mother, and the community is as clear as the likeness in other truths enunciated by the Gospel, but it does not seem that this particular comparison can find a basis in the text itself. If the beloved disciple is a symbol, it is because he is the type of disciple, of any disciple of Christ, but not because he represents the community. It must even be said that it is explicitly as an individual that John becomes the son of Mary. A relationship of mother to son is an individual relationship, and we understand that this individual character of the motherhood of Mary is very distinct. This motherhood will not possess its true nature and purpose unless it is established *in regard to each disciple personally* and in a certain manner as if he were the only one. The distinctive sign of maternal love is that it is given to each child individually, is interested in all the concrete details of his personal life, and gives the impression to each one of being loved as if he were the only one to receive affection and solicitude. If on Calvary Mary had been proclaimed mother of the community, we would have understood this motherhood in a more global sense, which would have been necessarily more vague. Since it was pronounced to a single disciple, the motherhood is granted to each one individually, with all the strength of an individualized correspondence of person to person.

The narrative does not actually suggest a corporate interpretation and does not show any trace of the notion of a unification of the faithful. It is certainly true that in the Old Testament, the idea of motherhood in the economy of salvation had been applied to Israel, to the Jewish community: Israel or Sion was looked upon as a mother, and the Jews were her children. This idea of maternity applied to the community will be used in the Apocalypse in the analogy of the woman in labor in whom we identify the symbol of the elect people or of the Church (Apoc. 12). Some exegetes have tried to recognize in Jesus' declaration to his mother the same idea of a maternity attributed to the community and disregard the historic person of Mary, seeing in her only the Judaic-Christian community.[4] But this stretches the text to an arbitrary interpretation and fails to see that Christ is really conferring upon his mother, present in flesh and blood, the universal maternity that, if he had simply followed certain indications of the Old Testament, he would have identified with the Jewish or Christian community. Here there is something new; the setting with its circumstances, has been well chosen to emphasize that motherhood is attached to the very person of Mary just as the motherhood of the Son of God had been attached to her person.

Furthermore, let us note that if we see Mary as mother of the community, we must show not that Mary represents the community, but that the beloved disciple represents it. Now he is not the type of the community but the type of each disciple considered individually and is a proof that every disciple individually becomes the son of Mary.

If we want to introduce the community into the episode, we must have recourse to elements that do not actually belong to the text. Therefore, this conclusion exceeds the perspective opened up by Saint John's narrative. Once we have determined the meaning of Christ's declaration, we examine its relationship with the establishment of the ecclesiastical community. Granted that Mary's motherhood was constituted individually for each disciple, nevertheless, it affects him at the same time as a member of the community. Since that motherhood is associated with the communication of the fruits of the redemption, it is intended to strengthen the unity of Christians, which is one of these fruits. Therefore, it contributes its share in building up the community of the Church, and we easily comprehend the fact that Christians' having only one mother binds them together more closely and contributes to the unity of the

Church. To make it more clear, let us say that the universal motherhood of Mary is first of all a result of the union of Christ and the life which he communicates to his disciples. Everyone receives as his mother the mother of Christ because everyone shares the life of Christ. Then this universal maternity is intended to strengthen and consolidate the unification of the disciples in Christ. Mary helps in uniting Christians. *Her motherhood is consequently both an effect and an instrument of the unity of Christ;* she is an expression of the unique life of Christ which circulates through the members of the Church, but also an agent in the establishment of a unified community.

4. Foundation of the Motherhood

Now that we have analyzed the nature and the extent of the motherhood attributed to Mary, we must make note of the foundation of this maternity as it results from the declaration of the Savior according to the circumstances in which it was pronounced. When Jesus said to Mary, "Woman, behold thy son," he asked his mother to consummate her maternal sacrifice. He gave her to understand that John would henceforth take his place with her. He was declaring to her that his departure from this earth was going to take place and that she must accept that difficult separation. We can measure all that the title "Woman" signified at that moment. The separation which this title, first used at Cana, had already made clear was now to reach its culminating point. To be called "Woman" meant that Mary was about to sacrifice her maternal affection completely. The words, "Behold thy son," could not leave any doubt of the extent of the sacrifice. Mary understood immediately that by receiving the beloved disciple as her child, she was accepting the death of her own son. We know that up to the moment of death, the close relatives of the dying person can retain hope, but that the agony of the sacrifice is imposed on them in all its fullness when they see their dear one breathe his last sigh. Even before giving up his soul, Christ asked his mother for the complete offering of that sacrifice. Acceptance of the motherhood of the beloved disciple meant acceptance of the loss of Jesus. It was, therefore, on that supreme sacrifice that the new maternity granted to Mary now rested.

We had already noted the enrichment brought to the soul of Mary by a new dignity as mother of men, a motherhood with limitless prospects since it included each and every one of Christ's disciples. Yet this enrichment implied a renunciation; we must not lose sight of the tragic impact of Jesus' declaration that required an extremely painful counterpart to the new motherhood. It is true that Mary becomes mother of the disciples because she is mother of Christ; but she becomes so not by a simple prolongation of her original maternity but by the sacrifice of that motherhood and the withdrawal of Christ from her maternal affection. *Therefore the new motherhood of Mary has a distinct place in the order of redemption* and is not merely a consequence of her role in the mystery of the Incarnation.

Christ's word to his mother is understood then in the light of other declarations such as "He who loses his life for my sake, will find it" (Matt. 10:39; Mark 8:35; Luke 9:24; 17:33). Mary must lose her only son in order to receive a motherhood over countless sons. Her collaboration in the acquisition of her universal motherhood has been far more profound than her collaboration in the fulfillment of her divine maternity. At the Annunciation an assent given with faith had been sufficient, while on Calvary a complete holocaust involving her whole being was required. Mary had to earn universal motherhood by the immolation of her maternal love. Undoubtedly, she received from Christ the new title, but she paid a high price for it. And this complete sacrifice helped to foster the new maternity in the depth of her soul.

"BEHOLD THY MOTHER."

After he has spoken to Mary and has proclaimed her new motherhood, Christ turns to the disciple and points out to him who is henceforth to be his mother. This second declaration was not necessary to establish the true motherhood of Mary and to make John really her son. But coming as a complement to the first declaration, it taught the beloved disciple the filial attitude that he must bear to Mary. To the maternal care of Mary must correspond the duty of a disciple: John is called upon to show Mary the affection and veneration that a child gives to his mother.

To understand better this second word of the Lord, we must realize that Mary's motherhood could have been planned as totally invisible. Since it is a maternity of the spiritual order, it could have been exercised in an entirely hidden manner that would have dispensed us from thinking of it and responding to it by conscious filial behavior. On the contrary, Christ manifests his will that the spiritual life of the disciple be animated by a disposition of filial love toward Mary. The reciprocal character of the relationship of a mother with her child must be expressed concretely. This manifestation of the will of the Savior is in accord with the general design of salvation, which requires men to respond to the advances of divine love. Just as we must adhere willingly to that love, we must correspond with a filial heart to the maternal solicitude of Mary.

The words, "Behold thy mother," can be considered *the principle of the Christian's devotion to the Blessed Virgin*. They suggest a spontaneity that befits such devotion since it is addressed to Mary as a mother and since the affection of a child for his mother wells up spontaneously. But in suggesting that spontaneous tenderness, the Gospel scene does not give a purely sentimental basis to devotion to Mary. The foundation is in the express will of Christ who establishes the motherhood of the Virgin as a part of his work of salvation. To show devotion to Mary is first of all to fulfill the will of the Savior and to try to enter fully into the execution of his plan of salvation.

"AND FROM THAT HOUR THE DISCIPLE TOOK HER INTO HIS HOME"

The words "from that hour" help to show that the Evangelist has grasped the solemn note of Christ's declaration. The moment of that declaration is an "hour" specially important in the carrying out of the mission of Jesus, an hour still more important than that of the first miracle at Cana because it coincides with the supreme hour of the Savior's death. This confirms that the new motherhood of

Mary forms part of the consummation of the sacrifice of redemption.

The mention of the hour is all the more noticeable here because ordinarily we would have expected the mention of the day rather than the moment. Furthermore, the beloved disciple did not immediately return home with Mary. He remained by the cross even after the last sigh of Jesus, because he was a witness of the blow of the lance. We may reasonably presume that he remained there until the body had been taken down and laid in the tomb. But the Evangelist says, "from that hour," to show us clearly that that very hour created new dispositions in the heart of John and his decision to make his home with Mary. Here an interior transformation manifests itself by the exterior act of taking Mary into his house; this transformation took place in the beloved disciple as soon as he heard the word, "Behold thy mother."

Father Braun has enumerated four possible translations of this sentence: "This disciple took her into his home"; "the disciple received her into his home"; "the disciple received her as his own"; "the disciple received her as his own property." He excludes the first translation, the most common, because the verb "took" indicates an act of protection. Now Mary was entrusted to the disciple not so much as a woman to be protected as a mother to be venerated. The fourth translation would likewise be excluded because it is a farfetched supposition better suited to inanimate objects than to a person; the text does not mean, therefore, that the disciple considered Mary as his own property. Father Braun agrees with the second and the third translation between which we do not have to choose because they have the same meaning. First of all, the disciple "received her into his home," means he welcomed Mary into his dwelling under his roof; further, he "received her as his own," because his action is not simply that of a material hospitality, but indicates a reception of Mary into his soul, among his spiritual possessions.[5]

We may wonder if it is not preferable to keep the common translation while retaining the advantage of Father Braun's remarks for a more developed exegesis. The verb, *take,* is not contrary to the spirit of the context if we recognize it in the active and initiative role of the disciple who, after the declaration of Jesus, invites Mary to come to his home and does not wait for Mary to present herself there in order to welcome her. The translation, "the disciple took her into his home," does not strictly imply an act of protection; it means a welcome, but a welcome which the disciple offers. It is John who makes the move and who invites the Virgin; it is he who leads her into his home.

On the other hand, "into his home," would seem preferable to "to his own" for it is the more ordinary meaning of the Greek expression used here by Saint John. ("to his own house" — John 16:32; "he came unto his own" — 1:11).[6] This meaning most naturally suits the situation. It seems too farfetched to interpret the meaning of the text to be that the disciple received Mary among his goods or possessions, that is to say, among his spiritual goods or into his soul. We can truly judge that Mary was welcomed into the soul of the disciple by the fact that Mary is welcomed into his home, but we must not try at all cost to read it into the words themselves. In the words we read merely that John took Mary into his home, and we know of no more beautiful symbol of intimacy between the disciple and his mother.

The conduct of the disciple in regard to Mary is all the more significant because it seems to duplicate an initial action of the Master in regard to John. In all probability, John had been one of the two disciples who had left John the Baptist to follow Jesus at the start of the public life. We recall that they had begun to walk behind the Master in silence. To the question, "What is it you seek?" they answered, "Rabbi, where dwellest thou?" They received an invitation into the dwelling of Christ, "Come and see." "They came and saw where he was staying; and they remained with him that day" (John 1:38-39). In mentioning this recollection, we divine the importance that John attached to the first meeting. The first contact with Christ had been brought about under the form of hospitality offered by him, and John's reception into Jesus' dwelling had been the symbol of the intimacy which was henceforth going to bind the disciple to the Master. Later, moreover, when the Savior will want to express the enduring intimacy which he wishes to establish with his disciples, he will use the simile of habitation declaring that he will abide in them as they will abide in him; with the Father he will come to him who observes the commandments and will make his abode with him (John 15:4; 14:23).

It is now the privilege of the beloved disciple to offer to the mother of Christ hospitality, a symbol of complete and enduring intimacy, which had come to John as primary proof of Christ's love.

And since his attitude is typical of a disciple toward Mary, we learn this universal truth that, after the departure of Christ from this world, *intimacy with him implies for the Christian a filial intimacy with Mary*. According to the divine plan and order of spiritual life, every disciple, whoever he may be, must take Mary as his mother.

This attitude responds to the will of the Savior and, however little we reflect on it, we see that it is a simple manifestation of a fundamental principle of Christian life, according to which each of us must relive personally the very life of Christ. There can be no such life without a filial love for Mary. The honor which was granted to the beloved disciple to represent Christ, in a certain way, in the eyes of Mary is an honor granted to every Christian, who must conform his conduct to that of Christ, to verify his image in himself and consequently to act as a son toward the mother of Jesus who has become his mother. To take Mary to his own is part of the ideal of the life of a Christian.

II. Illustration of the Narrative by Other Scriptural Passages

Are there any references to other scriptural passages in the episode? First of all, we must acknowledge that the text does not contain any explicit reference, and the Evangelist does not, as in other episodes, cite any scriptural passage that he considers is being fulfilled.

This statement has not, however, discouraged exegetes like Father Gaechter and Father Braun. They point out that in that section of Saint John's Gospel which relates the crucifixion and death of Christ (19:17-34), the author is very careful to show in a series of individual facts the fulfillment of the prophecies. At three separate places, con-

cerning the distribution of garments, the thirst quenched
with vinegar, and the blow of the lance, this statement is
repeated: "That the Scripture might be fulfilled." This
particular episode is thus framed within characteristic facts
which the Evangelist sees as a verification of scriptural passages. Since immediately after the twofold declaration of
Jesus to Mary and to the beloved disciple we are told that
Christ was aware that all had been consummated, Father
Gaechter and Father Braun think that the author was likewise disclosing the fulfillment of a prophecy in this episode.
What prophecy? If we review all the prophecies that concern the mother of the Messiah, only the Protogospel can
be considered.[7] Besides, it is only in the passage from Genesis
(3:15) that we find a role assigned to the "Woman," a role
which seems to have its fulfillment in her whom Christ
when dying calls "Woman." The Evangelist would then
have considered the scene as fulfillment of the prediction of
the Protogospel which announced the struggle between the
woman and the serpent.[8]

Father Braun confirms this interpretation by the great
role that the combat between Christ and Satan plays in the
Gospel of Saint John; on Calvary the victory is won over
the "Prince of this world."[9] To those who object that there
is no reference to the text of Genesis, he answers that the
Evangelist has not mentioned the relationship between Eve
and Mary because this relationship would force itself on the
readers and would be understood. The presence of Mary, of
the "Woman," near the Messiah at the hour of the victory
over the demon would reveal her to be the "Woman" spoken
of in Genesis.[10]

This exegesis has not failed to stir up criticism.[11] In fact, it appears very difficult to prove the intention of the Evangelist to make any reference to the Protogospel. Certainly the Evangelist considered the scene as forming part of the fulfillment of the Messianic mission of Jesus. But it is not certain that he saw in it the fulfillment of a scriptural passage since, unlike the preceding and following episodes, this passage makes no mention that the Scripture has been fulfilled. Why this omission if not because he did not find any text of the Old Testament adapted to the scene? If he had had in mind any likeness, he would certainly not have neglected to indicate it, since he was very careful to mention the fulfillment of the Scripture in each instance.

It is not, then, to the Evangelist that we must look for an intentional scriptural allusion. The Evangelist had realized that the episode had a wider importance than its immediate significance because the action of Jesus had a Messianic bearing. He must attribute a symbolic value to the declaration of Jesus; but nothing indicates that his intention went beyond that. On the other hand, Christ's intention is more complete and takes account of Mary's place in the whole plan of redemption. It is to that intention of Christ that we must attach a similarity to other texts of Scripture, provided these texts do offer an objective basis of sufficient agreement. We retain only the passages where we observe a really characteristic similarity with the proclamation, "Woman, behold thy son."

THE SORROWFUL CHILDBEARING

Before considering a comparison with the Old Testament or with the theological concepts of the Evangelist, it is important to find out whether Jesus himself did not make a declaration which sheds light on the meaning of the word addressed to his mother. Now we find in the Gospel of Saint John a very significant reference placed in the mouth of the Savior on the eve of his death, at the moment which immediately precedes his passion: "A woman about to give birth has sorrow, because her hour has come. But when she has brought forth the child, she no longer remembers the anguish for her joy that a man is born into the world" (John 16:21). When he proposes this picture, the Master does not apply it to Mary; he uses it to explain to the disciples how the sadness which they will experience and are already experiencing in hearing him make his farewells, will be turned into joy. But although there is no express application to Mary, certainly the mother of Jesus formed part of the group of disciples who were going to be a prey to sorrow and pass from sadness to joy. More than all the others, Mary verified this picture of the woman who is about to give birth, because more than all the others she would be subject to grief at the time of the passion, and then filled with joy by the triumph of her son.

Moreover, by virtue of the will of the Savior, Mary fulfills in a unique way this figure which serves to describe the disciples' participation in the Passion. In her, there is not only passage from grief to joy, as in the others, but there is a true childbearing. It is the childbearing brought about by the declaration, "Woman, behold thy son." When he pronounced this word, Christ made Mary *the woman in whom was fulfilled in an integral way participation in the work of redemption by a sorrowful childbearing followed by joy.* The figure proposed the evening before becomes full reality in

[202]

Mary, and it would be difficult to claim that this realization was not according to the intention of the Master.

Now it was at the same time the fulfillment of a rather frequent figure of speech in the Old Testament; the sorrows which would mark the day of the Lord had been compared to the anguish of the woman in labor, and they were sometimes linked with the hope of deliverance and of salvation (Isa. 13:8; 21:3; 26:7). Regarding the Messianic coming of the Son of man, Jesus speaks of the pangs of child-bearing and in this he follows a Jewish tradition (Matt. 24:8; Mark 13:8). The figure was, therefore, associated with that of the Messianic salvation. But in the Old Testament, the woman in labor represented Sion or the Jewish people. When Christ, in his farewell address at the Last Supper, recalls the figure, he applies it vaguely to the disciples as a whole. On Calvary, on the other hand, it is Mary who fulfills individually in a unique and perfect way what had been said of all in general. She, therefore, eminently verifies in herself what the Old Testament had said of Israel and what Jesus himself had declared of all the disciples in their share in the work of redemption.

It is not necessary to have recourse to the Apocalypse to discern *a relationship between Mary and the Church* from the point of view of their role in redemptive suffering. In chapter twelve of the Apocalypse, the woman who gives birth in sorrow seems to be, according to the perspective of the Old Testament summarily adapted to the New, "the people of God who in suffering, must engender the Messiah and his race."[12] Strictly, it is not the Church, but the people from whom the Messiah issued; nor is it Mary. On the contrary, if we take what Christ said about the woman

[203]

in labor, we apply it first to the group of disciples, that is to say, to the Church in formation and then find full and ideal fulfillment in the single person of Mary. If the whole Church is called to share in the redemption in suffering and in joy, it is Mary who participates in a perfect manner. She is the model of "compassion," of the association in the suffering of Christ crucified as well as in the joy of Christ glorious.

Furthermore, if we continue our theological reflection on the comparison of the two texts, we see that Mary is not only the one who verifies an interior disposition which must be that of all the Church; in the sorrowful compassion, she is more than a model for the disciples; she brings them forth. Therefore she possesses the dominant function in the Church which is that of a mother; she has an active mission in the generation of disciples and consequently in the very generation of the Church. She exercises a *certain causality over the constitution of the Church,* and it would not be enough to consider her the most eminent member of the Church or the example for all the disciples to follow. Through her sorrowful childbearing on Calvary, she played a unique role in the origin of the Church, a role which belongs to her alone.

Let us remark the very close connection between her role and that of Christ. In her, the image of the woman in labor would suggest an independent action, a work accomplished only by the woman. But Christ has applied this image to the participation which the disciple would take in the Passion of redemption. He envisaged the suffering of the disciples, therefore, not as independent but as founded on his. Likewise their joy will come from their association in the triumph of the glorious Messiah. This completely corresponds with

Mary's situation at the foot of the cross; she suffers from the affliction of her son. Therefore, the childbearing in anguish is not an independent action in Mary; it is a childbearing which, like the anguish itself, is produced by participation in the suffering of the Savior and is entirely based on it. Therefore, when we spoke of a causality of Mary in the origin of the Church, expressed by the generation of disciples, we did not by any means intend to separate that causality from the more fundamental action of Christ. In the person of Mary, that causality has an aspect which is her own, that of maternity, but it rests integrally on the saving power of Christ. We have emphasized the fact that Christ makes Mary the mother of the disciple, saying, "Woman, behold thy son." Christ, therefore, is the primary author of the childbearing.

Although it is unique, Mary's role is carried out, therefore, only through participation with that of the Savior. This close association between the mother and the son is still further corroborated by a detail of Jesus' declaration in regard to the woman about to give birth. She "has sorrow because her hour has come." It is then a suffering commanded by the divine plan and specially coordinated with the destiny of the Messiah because the expression, "his hour has come," is used elsewhere to designate specifically the hour of Christ's death (John 8:30; 7:30; 13:1). We saw that when Jesus said, "The hour has come," he was referring to the hour of his supreme glorification, according to the mind of Saint John, already envisioned on the cross. The hour of the woman in labor is, therefore, parallel with the hour of the Messiah. The perfect coincidence in Mary's case is very striking. At the moment of expiring, Jesus proclaims Mary's anguished childbearing of the disciple. Mary's hour has, therefore, been fixed by the hour of the Savior; it is *one and the same hour*.

Furthermore, if the glorification of the Messiah transpires in his exaltation on the cross, it is the same with Mary's joy which springs forth, so to speak, from her anguish. In the words, "Behold thy son," are indissolubly bound together the sacrifice of losing Jesus and the happiness of having a new child. Out of the suffering is born a pure and cloudless joy. The motive that the Savior assigns to the happiness of the woman who gives birth is revealing: it is "the joy that a man is born into the world." Christ does not say the joy of seeing her child; he stresses the disinterested nature of this happiness, as the mother rejoices not merely for having a child, but for giving a child to the world. The existence of a human being brings her happiness. Such is, indeed, the disposition of Mary, whose maternity on Calvary is completely disinterested. When Jesus speaks to her, he calls her "Woman," for she is a mother who loses her maternity, who sees her son dying. From the simple point of view of her affections, Mary cannot rejoice in the exchange nor be satisfied to have John as a son in place of Jesus. Her maternal joy could be established only on a higher disinterested plane, the *joy that a Christian is born into the world*, a new son of God born of her in the image of Christ.

THE VIRGINAL CHILDBEARING

The anguished childbearing of the disciple, which took place at the summit of Christ's life on Calvary, accords with the virginal childbearing for it is immediately apparent that

[206]

Mary becomes the mother of John because she was the mother of Jesus and because, in a way, John succeeds Christ as child of Mary. To understand this childbirth of the disciple, we must then go back to the childbearing of Christ himself.

Let us recall how that childbearing of Jesus is narrated in the Prologue of Saint John's Gospel. To all those who received him and who believed in his name the Word "gave the power of becoming sons of God who were born not of blood, nor of the will of the flesh, nor of the will of man, but of God" (John 1:12-13). On the divine filiation of the Savior rests his power to communicate to others the quality of sons of God. Christ is, in fact, "born of God" and his divine filiation has been manifested in the virginal birth. That he was not born according to the laws of human generation reveals the divine origin of his generation, a proof of a transcendent filiation. The quality of Son of God is thus linked, in its manifestation, with that of the son of the Virgin.

The scene on Calvary proves that Christ wishes to communicate the quality of Son of God precisely through the quality of son of the Virgin. Through his death, he merits for men the dignity of adopted sons of the Father, and when he returns glorious on the day of his resurrection, he will allude to the new condition of his disciples, to their divine filiation. He expressly calls the disciples his brothers and addresses them, "I ascend to my Father and your Father" (John 11:17) to indicate that the first fruit of the redemption is a special paternity of the heavenly Father in their regard. But as in him Christ verified indissolubly filiation toward the Father and filiation toward Mary, he wishes that his disciples unite the quality of sons of God with that of sons of Mary. His virginal birth had signified his divine filiation; the birth of disciples by the Virgin Mary will signify their adoptive filiation with the Father. By declaring the beloved disciple a son of Mary, he confers on him a visible title of his invisible filiation with the Father.

Such is the greatness of Mary's universal maternity; the virginal childbearing on Calvary is the sign of a childbearing operated by God himself. The motherhood of the Virgin *is a manifestation of the paternity of God over all Christians.*

Let us add that the sorrowful character of the childbearing comes in a certain manner to strengthen its virginal character. Virginity consists, in fact, in opening itself to the divine action by renouncing human power and the human desire to give birth. Now in the sacrifice of Calvary Mary renounces her human desire for motherhood and all human power over her son; for her the death of Jesus is suppression of her human fecundity as mother. The renunciation that had been formerly implied in her virginal consecration is, therefore, carried to its highest degree. *As she stands by the cross, there is within her a consummation of her virginity.* And because her first maternity had been granted to her after her offering of virginity, her second maternity is likewise granted in consequence of a virginity consummated in pain. By accepting the human annihilation of her maternity, Mary permits God to operate a new motherhood within her. Because she has renounced the human demands of maternal longing, she participates intimately in the fruitful paternity of God.

THE NEW EVE

We have seen how Father Braun had introduced into his interpretation a reference from the Evangelist to the Protogospel. He makes special note that the victory of the Messiah over the demon is fulfilled on Calvary, a victory announced in the prediction of the struggle between the serpent and the woman's seed. Much earlier, E. C. Hoskyns had proposed several points of comparison between Genesis and the Gospel of Saint John to shed light on the word of Jesus to his mother: the "woman" considered as mother, the new creation by the Word, the new birth and formation of Mary from the side of the new Adam during the sleep or death of the latter.[13]

Of all possible relationships, we retain only that which results from an analogy that is characteristic and appears to be part of the divine plan, even if the Evangelist is not cognizant of it. In the scene we are studying, nothing recalls to us the struggle of the Messiah with the demon or the serpent.[14] It is not a question now of a new birth from Mary, but rather of a new maternity of Mary in correlation with the new sonship of Christians. If we read the opening of Genesis, we discern only one feature that appears to agree conspicuously with the significance of this episode and sheds any new light on it. It is the interpretation of the name, Eve, connected, according to a popular etymology, with the word, "life." After the sanction had been pronounced on the guilty ones and God had told the woman that she would bring forth children in sorrow, we read this sentence, "And Adam called the name of his wife, Eve, because she was the mother of all the living" (Gen. 3:20).

We recognize in these words the meaning of the declaration made by Christ. On Calvary, it is the Son of man who calls Mary, "Woman," in view of establishing her as *mother of all the living in the order of grace*. The text of Genesis particularly helps us to understand that the title "Woman" does not denote merely the sacrifice of her maternal affection which Mary must offer, but indicates also that she is a source of life by that sacrifice. In calling her "Woman," Christ wishes to regard her as a woman in the full sense of the word, according to that etymological meaning of "life" which had been applied originally to the first woman. He recognizes in her the superior nobility of a spiritual motherhood, of a fecundity in the realm of true life. The true Eve was Mary. The old Eve had been merely a figure of universal motherhood in the order of corporal life, in itself, likewise, only a figure of eternal life.

On Calvary, the history of the world began again, or rather began. Christ became the principle of life for all his disciples, and Mary was established by him as the ideal woman, the fullness of feminine potentiality, that is to say, a mother with the mission of transmitting divine life to men through spiritual generation.

The text of Genesis does not only invite us to recognize in Mary, associated with Christ, a new origin of humanity. It also enlightens us on the meaning of the sorrowful childbearing which took place on Calvary. Eve had become mother of all the living by the childbearing in anguish, stipulated as punishment for sin. There is then a relation between sin and the sorrowful childbearing on Calvary. Certain texts of the Old Testament that applied to the Jewish people the figure of the woman in labor emphasized the terrible character of these sufferings as a sign of the divine wrath in chastisement of sin (Isa. 13:8; Jer. 13:21; 22:23). But other texts above all brought to light the relationship between these sufferings and salvation, with imminent deliverance. (Mich. 9:9-10; Isa. 66:7). When he made use of the metaphor, Jesus stressed this last idea, insisting on the fecundity of grief and the joy that would result from it. Therefore, according to that word of the Savior, it is necessary to understand the relation between sin and sorrowful childbearing in the wider perspective of the redemption. Christ took on himself death which had been the penalty pronounced against Adam because of his sin; but, in assuming it, he transformed its meaning since he made it an instrument of redemption. Likewise, Mary, on Calvary, in spite of her innocence and her exemption from all sin, was subjected to the pangs of childbearing, the pain which had been pronounced as the penalty against Eve after the fall. But she had changed the significance of that anguished labor by taking it as an instrument of redemption. On the contrary, in that pain, which was to mark the victory of sin over woman, was revealed a triumph of woman over sin, a sacrifice which contributed to the remission of sin.

In the declaration, "Woman, behold thy son," the complete meaning of the sentence was revealed: "In sorrow shalt thou bring forth children," at the same time that this announcement of the Old Testament found its most sublime fulfillment. The sorrowful childbearing, instead of being a chastisment for the fault and a sign of the servitude of woman, was *a reparation of that fault and a sign of the deliverance of mankind.*

The narrative of Genesis, which draws our attention to

[211]

the importance of the role of Eve in the initial drama, enlightens us further on *the importance of Mary's role* in the
decisive drama of the redemption. By placing Eve beside
Adam and emphasizing their joint role in the fall and its
consequences, it bids us understand better the importance
of Mary's presence beside Christ crucified and the con-
junction of her mission with that of her son. This conjunc-
tion does not keep it from being dependent and subordinate.
It is Adam who calls Eve the mother of all the living and
confers upon her the claim to motherhood. This dominant
role, Adam possessed already because Eve had been drawn
from his side and she had been made subject to him. Likewise, it is Christ who confers on Mary her quality of universal mother by calling her to be mother of the beloved
disciple. Mary is subordinated to the Savior and draws the
whole merit of her sacrifice from the sacrifice of her son.
Nevertheless, in the figure of Eve placed beside Adam,
she is true collaborator of Christ in his work of regenera-
tion of men. With the Savior, through her anguish, she
gives birth to the new mankind.

Such are the three aspects of the episode of Calvary
which the narrative of Genesis makes more clear. First of
all, the universal motherhood, the ideal accomplishment of
the vocation of woman: Mary is called Woman because she
becomes the mother of all the living. Then the sorrowful
childbearing in its relation with sin: this penalty of childbearing Mary takes on herself in order to make it a work
of redemption, of supreme moral nobility. Finally, the association of woman with man, an association which does
not exclude dependence: Mary, whose sacrifice draws its
substance from the redeeming sacrifice of Jesus, as "Woman"

is the associate of the one man or rather of the Son of man, his collaborator in the work of salvation and in the generation of the sons of God.

Epilogue

The Mystery of Pentecost

We leave the Gospel to enter the Acts of the Apostles, the history of the Church. At the outset of this history, we again find the name of Mary, in a very laconic mention, without any other indication of word or act; nevertheless, it is a significant mention, if beyond its literal meaning we place it in relationship with what the Gospels have given us. Mary is present at the beginning of the Church as she had been present at the beginning of the Gospel, at the beginning of the hidden life, and at the beginning and end of the public life.

The text of Saint Luke would certainly allow us to conclude that in the group gathered in the Cenacle, Mary enjoyed a very special prominence since she is the only one named among the women (Acts 1:14). The fact that soon they will choose a "brother of the Lord" as first bishop of Jerusalem reveals the esteem that was accorded to the family of Jesus and lets us think that a rank of pre-eminence in the community was given to his mother. But the part to be played by Mary at Pentecost cannot be based on familial rights. Since it was the last phase of the work of redemption which was going to set the Church in action, it was *by right*

[214]

of collaborator in the plan of salvation that the Blessed Virgin could specially intervene in it.

First of all, the Gospel of Saint Luke has clearly shown *the unique relationship which binds Mary to the Holy Spirit.* The salient point of the Angel Gabriel's message is the annunciation of the coming of the Holy Spirit who will bring about the virginal conception. If we compare this event of the Incarnation with that of Pentecost, the analogy seems to claim the cooperation of Mary in both cases. If the Blessed Virgin was called to collaborate in the miraculous intervention of the Holy Spirit for the birth of Christ, would it not be likely that the reason of her presence in the Cenacle was to insure collaboration in the miraculous intervention of the Holy Ghost in the formation of the Church?

The mystery of the Visitation confirms that role. Carried by Mary, Christ for the first time had diffused the Holy Spirit by a sudden and extraordinary communication, to the point that we can discern in the charism given to Elizabeth the figure of the charism which would be given to the apostles. Already Elizabeth had been "filled" with the Holy Spirit, had felt the shock of a trembling with joy, and had been specially gifted with the faculty of speaking under divine inspiration. Now Elizabeth had recognized that the shock had been produced in her through contact with Mary, when Mary's voice had reached her. Are we not right, therefore, in thinking that, if Christ wishes to spread the Holy Spirit over the whole community, he will certainly do it with some cooperation from his mother?

The episode of Cana reveals another title to the cooperation of Mary in the mystery of Pentecost: *it is the*

Virgin who, by her prayer, provoked the first manifestation of the Messianic power of the Savior. Here, there is a definitive manifestation of that power since the sending of the Holy Spirit is the work of Christ triumphant, established in heavenly glory. This manifestation is prepared for by the prayer of the community, and it is on the occasion of that common prayer that Saint Luke mentions the presence of Mary. For the Virgin, that prayer is certainly the extension of the petition of Cana, and we may well recognize in it a unique privilege of efficacy.

The quality of cooperatrix in the sacrifice of redemption constitutes another essential motive of collaboration in the mystery of the effusion of the Holy Spirt, for this effusion is the fruit of the sacrifice. It is the outpouring of the glorious saving power of which Christ has taken possession in consequence of his complete despoliation on Calvary. Mary had been very intimately associated in that sacrifice, and she had even had the role of being the first to offer her son for his sorrowful destiny in view of the rise or "resurrection" of many. It is this spiritual rise or "resurrection" which is going to be produced as an effect of Pentecost. The Virgin of the Presentation in the Temple, united with the cross of Jesus, is then only completing her mission by intervening in the mystery of Pentecost.

A fourth aspect of her mission further justifies and makes clear the reason for her presence in the Cenacle. By virtue of her association in the sacrifice, Mary received on Calvary *the quality of mother of Christians.* This mission as mother implies that she performs a role in the formation and development of Christian life in each individual. Now the gift of the Holy Ghost is the most fundamental gift, the source of Christian life. The Virgin, consequently, has a maternal role to play in granting this gift. We repeat what we said earlier in regard to the analogy between the Incarnation and Pentecost. When Mary became mother of Christ through the operation of the Holy Spirit, by an analogous operation, she was to become mother of Christians.

All these titles of Mary which characterize a unique and privileged collaboration in the divine plan of salvation confer a unique and privileged significance on her presence in the Cenacle. It is true that the Acts of the Apostles do not give us any light on this significance since the presence of the mother of Jesus is merely mentioned in company with the apostles, the women, and the "brothers of Jesus." But we cannot abstract from all that the Gospel has told us of Mary. In the Cenacle, Mary continues the mission in which we see her engaged from the time of the Annunciation to the closing of the public life of Christ. This mission of maternity and of coredemption we can express in a word through relation to Pentecost: the Virgin is in the midst of the disciples as mother of the *Church in formation*. It is through her, who had once represented to the Angel Gabriel the Church to come, that the prayer of the whole community must mount to heaven. It is by her maternal cooperation that the Holy Spirit will be poured forth throughout the world.

Notes

Introduction

1. We cite in particular F. M. Braun, *La Mere des fideles* (Tournai, 1953); P. Gaechter, *Maria im Erdenleben* (Innsbruck, 1953); S. Lyonnet, *"Le recit de l'Annonciation et la maternite divine de la sainte Vierge,"* in *L'Ami du clerge,* 66 (1956), 33-48; R. Laurentin, *Structure et Theologie de Luc I-II* (Paris, 1957).

Chapter 1

1. For a detailed analysis of the Semitic marks in the narrative, see J. G. Machen, *The Virgin Birth of Christ* (New York, 1932), pp. 62-118. He shows that the narative is from the hand of St. Luke and that it has, nevertheless, a strong Palestinian color which supposes a Palestinian origin or source.

2. In his prologue (1:1-4), Luke notes the care he took to report the facts faithfully after serious investigation of the sources. Therefore, while claiming that the literary style of the first two chapters of Saint Luke show the influence of a *midrash* (commentary of a scriptural passage), Laurentin stresses their historic value (*op. cit.,* pp. 96f.).

3. Prat affirms that "this honor was never repeated," (*Jesus Christ* [Paris, 1938], p. 59). According to Strack-Billerbeck, cited particularly by Gaechter (*op. cit.,* p. 20), the priest designated by lot could never be designated again until all the other priests of his class had received the same privilege.

Notes

As the priests were very numerous, a new designation was practically impossible.

4. M. J. Lagrange, *Evangile selon Saint Luc* (Paris, 1921), p. 13.

5. *Ibid.*, p. 26. To relate the words "of the house of David" to Mary, we could not rely on the fact that they might have been inserted at a later redaction, in the course of successive stages of composition. If we presume that they have been added by an intermediary relator or by St. Luke, they have been added beside the name of Joseph. If they had been intended to indicate Mary's origin, the words, εξ οἰκου Δαυίδ would have been placed after παρθενον and not after Ιωσήφ.

Nor can we claim that relating these words to Joseph makes superfluous the indication given later of the origin of Joseph as "being of the house and the family of David" (2:4). There was, in fact, a reason for the Evangelist to repeat this mention of origin; it explained the journey to Bethlehem.

Finally the parallel with Elizabeth, whose origin is noted in 1:5, does not furnish a motive for referring these words to Mary, precisely because it is a parallel which includes a contrast, made very evident by the mention of Elizabeth's virtue and the absence of such mention in regard to Mary.

We must then give these words their natural meaning and agree that the qualification "of the house of David" concerns Joseph. The Evangelist had a motive in citing this origin because the angel is going to present the child Jesus, as son of David. Now, as the genealogies of Matthew (1:6) and Luke (3:13) show, it was through Joseph that Jesus was descended from David.

A theological reflection can, nevertheless, show the importance of this omission of all mention of Mary's origins: first, the absolute freedom of the divine choice which does not stop for any consideration of racial titles; secondly, the relation of this mystery of Mary's origin with her divine maternity. While Joseph must bear witness to the legal descent of Jesus, Mary is the Virgin who must be witness to the divine origin of her child.

6. The fact that the Gospel of Saint Luke appears less frankly

universalist in the first two chapters, according to the remark of Laurentin (*op. cit.*, pp. 12, 102), does not constitute an objection to the affirmation of a universalist orientation in the very elements of the setting of the Annunciation since we do not wish to attribute this orientation to the mind of the Evangelist.

7. *Art. cit.;* also, "χαιρε χεχαριτωμενη" in *Biblica*, 20 (1939), 131-141.

8. *"Le recit de l'Annonciation . . . ,"* 40.

9. *"L'Annonciation (Luc I, 26-38),"* in *Nouvelle Revue Theologique,* 66 (1939), 797, n. 8. Cauppens observes that an invitation to rejoice would not have prevented trouble due to Mary's humility (*De Mariologia biblica* [Turin, 1951], p. 62).

10. *Art. cit.,* in *Biblica* (1939), 134.

11. On the meaning of this word, let us cite the analysis of M. de Tuya in his article, *"Valoracion exegetico-teologica del 'Ave, gratia plena,' "* in *Ciencia Tomista,* 43 (1956), 9-27, 28.

12. *Op. cit.,* p. 28.

13. Confer A. Medebielle, *"Annonciation,"* in *Dictionnaire de la Bible, Suppl.* I, 283: "The Greek verbs ending in ὀω all have a meaning of abundance, growth, plenitude; αιματόω to cover with blood; θαυμαστόω to fill with stupor; σποδόω to cover with ashes. We must specially note that this meaning of abundance and of plenitude is in εχαριτωσεν from Ephesians 1:6; the grace that God has granted in his beloved Son is a rich, overflowing grace.

14. *Op. cit.,* p. 28.

15. This is the argument proposed by M. de Tuya (*art. cit.,* 15). It invokes, likewise, the plenitude of the Holy Spirit attributed to Saint Stephen in the Acts of the Apostles (8:55).

16. This point particularly is brought out by Holzmeister in his article, *"Dominus tecum, Lc. I, 28,"* in *Verbum Domini,* 23

Notes

(1943), 232-237, 257-262. He reviews all the parallel texts of the Old Testament.

17. Lyonnet observes that Saint John, in reproducing the Messianic prophecy fo Zachary, replaced "rejoiced" with "fear not" (12:15). The absence of fear is the feeling that suits the coming of the Messiah (*La recit dell'Annonciation, p. 40*).

18. *Op. cit.*, pp. 119-168.

19. *"Bermerkungen zu Lk. I, 26-38,"* in *Biblische Zeitschrift,* 7 (1909), 30-48.

20. D. Haugg, *Das erste biblische Marienwort* (Stuttgart, 1938), pp. 36-56, 61-73; Gaechter, *op. cit.*, pp. 92-98; "The Chronology from Mary's Betrothal to the Birth of Christ," in *Theological Studies,* 2 (1941), 159-162.

21. *Op. cit.*, p. 40.

22. *Art. cit.*, 161.

23. *"Maria und das christliche Jungfraulichkeitsideal,"* in *Geist und Leben,* 23 (1950), 411-425.

24. *"L'annonce à Marie,"* in *Revue Biblique,* 63 (1956), 346-374.

25. We note particularly the criticism of the opinion of Landersdorger by Lagrange (*op. cit.*, p. 30); the answer of Holzmeister to Haugg's book in his article, *"Quomodo fiet istud, quoniam virum non cognosco?"* in *Verbum Domini,* 19 (1939), 70-75; Neubert's answer to Gaechter in his article, *"La chronologie depuis les fiancailles de Marie jusqu' à la naissance du Christ,"* in *Marianum,* 4 (1942), 10-20; the article of P. B. Brodmann, *"Mariens Jungfräulichkeit nach Lk. I, 34 in der Auseinandersetzung von heute,"* in *Antonianum,* 30 (1955), 37-44; P. B. Leurent's article, *"La consécration de Marie à Dieu,"* in *La Revue d'Ascétique et de Mystique,* 31 (1955), 255-268. This last article gives an overall picture of tradition on the subject.

26. *Lerecit de l'Annonciation,* p. 42.

27. Confer particularly Strack-Billerbeck, *Kommentar zum NT aus Talmud und Midrash*, II, 398, where we find a rabbinical text from R. Cijja (280), a text invoked by Holzmeister (*art. cit.*, 71) and Brodmann (*art. cit.*, 38).

28. *De Spec. Leg.*, III, 12.

29. *Op. cit.*, p. 33.

30. Confer Gaechter, *op. cit.*, p. 97.

31. *De vita contemplativa*, 21-90. Lagrange wonders if the description of the sect of the Therapeutes is not an "allegorical fiction" in which Philon would have expressed his own ideal (*Le judaisme avant Jesus Christ* [Paris, 1931], p. 586). Lyonnet remarks that such imaginary description would be highly improbable and that in any case the passage shows that "a Jew, contemporaneous with the Virgin could conceive an ideal of feminine chastity" (*Le recit de l'Annonciation*, p. 42, n. 10).

32. G. Vermes brought the meaning of the prohibition, found in *Combat des fils de lumiere contre les enfants des tenebres* (VII, 3-4), that forbade the women to go into a camp during the war; the sons of light are associated with the heavenly host and should live in an angelic manner ("*Quelques traditions de Qumran*," in *Cahiers Sioniens*, 9 [1955], p. 42). Confer R. Lauentin, *op. cit.*, p. 179f.

33. For this meaning, as it has been understood in tradition, we refer to an article in *Nouvelle Revue Theologique*, 89 (1957), entitled "*Vierge entre les vierges*," 463-467. Certain pages of this article are here included.

34. G. Lambert associates the presence of the serpent with the pagan worship of fecundity that made women invoke the serpent for their fecundity instead of having recourse to Yahweh ("*Le drame du jardin d'Eden*," in *Nouvelle Revue Theologique*, 76 (1954), 1046f.). H. Cazelles emphasizes also the importance of Genesis 6:1, where Eve says in regard to her first child, "I have acquired a son through Yahweh," in his article, "*Genese III, 15: Exegese contemporaine*," in *Etudes Mariales*, 14 (1956), 98. Gazelle states, "Eve is

then mother and mother with God." Let us add that even
in the case where it would be necessary to translate *qanah*
by produce rather than acquire, and admit an influence from
the Babylonian powem in which the goddess Arourou collaborates with the god Mardouk in the creation of mankind,
the idea expressed by the Yahviste that Eve brings forth a
child in collaboration with Yahweh would be only the more
evident.

35. On the meaning of this prophecy, confer J. Coppens, *"La
prophetie de la Almah, Isa. VII, 14-17,"* in *Ephemerides
Theologicae Lovanienses,* 28 (1952), 648-678.

36. Confer R. Bloch, *"Quelques aspects de la figure de Moise
dans la litterature rabbinique,"* in *Cahiers Sioniens,* 8 (1954),
245. R. Laurentin (*op. cit.,* p. 181), mentions besides this
rabbinical legend concerning Moses, the legend of the priest
Nir who had given up all relations with his wife from the
time that God had publicly taken him into his service. This
legend is probably of later date than the Gospel. Cf. Sahlin,
Der Messias und das Gottesvolk (Uppsala, 1945), p. 370.

37. *De sancta virginitate,* 4-6; PL:40, 398f.

38. On the parallelism between the faith of Abraham and that
of Mary, see E. D. O'Connor, "The Faith of Abraham and
the Faith of the Virgin Mary," in *The American Ecclesiastical Review,* 132 (1955), 232-238.

39. *Commentarii in quattuor Evangelistas* (Lyon, 1582), 880.

40. R. Laurentin, *Court traite de theologie mariale* (Paris, 1953),
p. 25. It is to this understanding of Mary that the author
attaches her trouble (Luke 1:29). But is this emotion not
anterior to the annunciation of the maternity? Besides, Saint
Luke relates this emotion to an interior interrogation and
not the perception of an unsetting truth.

41. *La recit de l'Annonciation,* p. 43-46. The article mentions
two other interesting uses of the verb, "overshadow," in the
Old Testament version of the Septuagint (Num. 9:18, 22;
II Par. 5: 7- 6:2).

42. *Art. cit.,* pp. 44-45.

43. Confer R. Laurentin, *Structure et Theologie de Luc,* I-II, p. 122.

44. Thus, Ceuppens invokes "a special light" by which Mary could comprehend the prophecies which regarded her son and know that she had been chosen for the dignity of Mother of God. At the same time he relies on the passages of the Old Testament announcing the divine character of the Messiah (*op. cit.,* p. 68).

45. This is the argument used by E. F. Sutcliffe to show that Mary did not know immediately that her son was God; see his article, "Our Lady and the Divinity of Christ," in *The Month* 180 (1945), 347-350. Laurentin would be inclined to see in Mary's lack of comprehension merely a momentary effect of the disconcerting proposal in regard to Jesus, which would have prevented any application in this circumstance of the knowledge of the divinity of Christ (*op. cit.,* 173). Is this not belittling the misunderstanding? If Mary had possessed this knowledge from the time of the Annunciation and had been simply hindered by the baffling turn of Jesus' words from making any application to it immediately, she would not have understood at the very moment, but she would have understood immediately afterwards. They would hardly have thought it worthwhile to mention a lack of understanding so transitory. The sentence, "They did not understand," does not seem justified unless the misunderstanding was more important, more profound; it calls forth a mystery.

46. R. Laurentin, *op. cit.,* p. 174.

47. In his commentary Lagrange indicates reasons to consider the quotation as a proof of the fulfillment of the text from Isaias (p. 260ff.).

48. Cf. S. Lyonnet, *Le recit de l'Annonciation,* pp. 42-43, n.1.

49. Such is the interpretation of Gaechter, *op. cit.,* pp. 144-147.

50. He is called, "Son of David," because by taking Mary he will place the Messiah in the line of David in her person,

Notes

by accepting him officially to be his father. This is what Matthew had especially in mind (M. J. Lagrange, *Evangile selon Saint Matthew* [Paris, 1923], p. 12f.).

Chapter II

1. On the preference to be given to the reading, "their purification," confer M. J. Lagrange, *Evangile selon Saint Luc*, p. 81.

2. The idea of a sacrificial offering is found in the word παραστῆσαι. Compare Luke 7:22 with Romans 12:1: "To present your bodies as a sacrifice, living, holy, pleasing to God."

3. Confer the remark of J. Coppens: "In the second narrative, it is not said that Manoe knew his wife. The text gives the impression that the mere manifestation of the angel of the Lord sufficed to make the woman conceive (*"La prophétie de la 'Almah,"* in *Ephemerides Theologicae Lovanienses,* 28 [1952], 655, n. 25).

4. We follow the reading και σου δε; on the interpretations which have been given of it, confer A. De Groot, *Die schmerzhafte Mutter und Gefährtin des göttlichen Erlosers in der Weissagung Simeons* (Kaldenkirchen, 1956), p. 79f.

5. ρομφαία is used in preference to μάχαιρα. There is no reason to insist too much on the distinction because elsewhere in Scripture the word ρομφαία seems to have the general meaning of sword. Cf. A. De Groot, *op. cit.,* p. 82.

6. In the Qumrân version, we also find the image of Verse 10: "Yahweh is pleased to grind him, and he transpierced him" (QIsa).

7. Among recent attempts to make very clear this liaison from the point of view of the coredemption, we cite particularly T. Gallus, *"De Sensu verborum Lc. II, 35 eorumque momento mariologico,"* in *Biblica,* 29 (1948), 220-239, and A. De Groot, *op. cit.,* pp. 97-114.

8. Gallus (*art. cit.,* 234) and De Groot (*op. cit.,* p. 89) prefer the pejorative meaning.

9. Confer De Groot in which various interpretations are verified (*ibid.*).

10. At least in the spiritual sense. In the New Testament the word ἀνάστασις designates the resurrection of the body; but here it is used in a more vague sense of rising in the spiritual order (Cf. Prov. 24:16).

11. Cf. the examples of this expression cited by Lagrange (*Op. cit.*, p. 97).

12. The reading ζητοῦμεν, although less well attested to by manuscripts, is preferred as more natural. The imperfect εζητουμεν could have been introduced to harmonize with εζητειτε which follows.

Chapter III

1. Confer H. Menoud, *L'Évangile de Jean d'après les recherches récentes* (Neuchâtel, 1943), p. 13. Menoud cites as typically Johannine the expressions, "Woman," and "my hour"; note, however, that they are found in the mouth of Jesus and are more characteristic of the language of the Master than of the Evangelist.

2. The comparison is made particularly by Boismard in *Du baptême à Cana* (Paris, 1956), p. 143f. Yet in spite of this comparison Boismard thinks that "the most natural interpretation of the text does not require a request for a miracle; it is not, however, definitely excluded."

3. F. M. Braun, *La Mère des fidèles* (Tournai, 1953), p. 179.

4. A. M. Brunet, "Les Noces de Cana," in *Études et Recherches,* VIII (Paris-Ottawa, 1952), p. 12.

5. *Ibid.*, 160-171.

6. *Ibid.*, 55.

7. *Ibid.*, 163f.

8. *Ibid.*, 168.

Notes

9. *Ibid.*, 170.

10. Correctly C. P. Ceroke insists upon the clue that these words of Mary constitute, in his article, "Jesus and Mary at Cana: Separation or Association," in *Theological Studies*, 17 (1956), 25.

11. J. A. Robilliard, *"Le vin manqua,"* in *La Vie Spirituelle*, 90 (1954), 35.

12. *Ibid.*, 40.

13. *In Ioannis Evangelium*, VIII, 9 and CXIX, 1; PL:35, 1455f. and 1950.

14. *Op. cit.*, p. 180f. Gaechter had already published his interpretation in an article, *"Maria in Kana (Jo. II, 1-11),"* in *Zeitschrift für katholische Theologie* (1931), 351-402.

15. F. M. Braun, *op. cit.*, p. 58.

16. In *Revue Biblique*, 41 (1932), 122.

17. Confer C. P. Ceroke, *art. cit.*, 4f.

18. It is characteristic of Saint John to consider the glorification not as a consequence of the death but in the death itself, as the use of the term "lift up" testifies (on the cross and in glory). Confer A. Vergte, *"L'Exaltation du Christ en croix selon le quatrième Évangile,"* in *Ephemerides Theologicae Lovanienses*, 28 (1952), 5-23.

19. C. Journet, *Les sept paroles de Jésus en croix* (Paris, 1952), p. 68.

20. R. Schnackenburg, *Das erste Wunder Jesu* (Fribourg-im-Br., 1951), p. 46.

21. The parallel has been used notably by O. Cullman, *Les Sacrements dans l'Évangile johannique* (Paris, 1951), p. 37.

22. In *Revue Biblique*, 61 (1954), 295, and in *Du baptême à Cana*, pp. 156-157. This is the interpretation of J. Knabenbauer, *Evangelium sec. Ioannem* (Paris, 1898), p. 120; of A. Durand, *Évangile de S. Jean* (Paris, 1930), p. 57; of

S. Grill, *"Jesus auf der Hochzeit zu Kana,"* in *Bibel und Liturgie*, 20 (1952-3), 335ff.; of J. Michl, *"Bemerkungen zu Joh. II, 4,"* in *Biblica*, 36 (1955), 492-509.

23. This remark has more weight because the Greek sentence begins with "not yet" and also because there is an insistence on this point.

24. *Art. cit.*, 34-37.

25. *"Les noces de Cana,"* in *La Vie Spirituelle*, 81 (1949), 155-162.

26. *Op. cit.*, p. 65. This is the interpretation the author seems to prefer after he first exposes Braun's exegesis.

27. *Art. cit.*, 33-34.

28. On this point the conclusion of Gaechter (*op. cit.*, p. 175) seems indisputable to us.

29. *Évangile selon saint Jean* (Paris, 1925), p. 56.

30. Thus, for example, in the *Iliad* it is the appellation addressed by Paris to Helen (III, 438) and by Hector to Andromache (VI, 441). Cf. Gaechter, *op. cit.*, p. 178.

31. J. Leal, *"La hora de Jesús, la hora de su Madre (Io. II, 4),"* in *Estudios Ecclesiasticos*, 26 (1952), 162. Ceroke remarks that to express this depreciative shade of meaning, the word "Woman" would have to be in the dative (to you who are a woman), rather than in the vocative (*art. cit.*, 29).

32. *Op. cit.*, p. 190.

33. Confer particularly A. Feuillet, *"Le Fils de l'homme de Daniel et la Tradition Biblique,"* in *Revue Biblique*, 60 (1953), 170-202, 321-346; Benoit, *"La Divinité de Jésus dans les Évangiles Synoptiques,"* in *Lumière et Vie*, 9 (1953), 63-71.

34. Confer J. Galot, *"L'énigme du 'Fils de l'homme,'"* in *Revue de Clergé Africain*, 12 (1957), 219.

35. Irenaeus, *Adversus Haereses*, III, 17, 7 (Harvey, II, 88).

Notes

36. J. Chrysostom, *In Iannem Homilia;* P.G.: 59, 130.

37. On the development of the doctrine of Mary's sanctity in the period of the Fathers, see G. Jouassard, *"Marie à travers la Patristique: Maternité divine, Virginité, Sainteté,"* in H. Du Manoir, *Maria,* I (Paris, 1949), 69-158.

38. After Loisy, O. Cullmann, *op. cit.,* p. 37; Braun, *op. cit.,* p. 65.

39. Braun, *op. cit.,* p. 66.

40. F. Quievreux, *"La maternité spirituelle de la Mère de Dieu dans saint Jean,"* in *Vie Spirituelle, Supplément* (1952), 106-109.

41. Braun appeals to a dispensation and believes that, after having affirmed the principle with clarity, Christ "remained free to satisfy the request of his mother not by obedience to her will as at Nazareth, but of his own volition with sovereign independence" (*op. cit.,* p. 64).

42. Gaechter, *op. cit.,* p. 192.

43. *Loc. cit.*

44. Confer on this subject the article by J. Levie, in *Nouvelle Revue Théologique,* 76 (1954), 432.

45. For the arguments in favor of this reading, we refer to Braun, *op. cit.,* pp. 33-38.

46. Cf. Phil. 2:6, where St. Paul, setting up Christ's attitude against that of Adam, declares that Christ did not consider equality with God something to be clung to, but received his glorification by becoming obedient even to the death of the cross. Mary's attitude at Cana is in conformity with that mode of acting by Christ.

47. St. John repeats the Precursor's words comparing Christ to the bridegroom (3:29).

48. Confer Osee 2:4-18; Ezech. 16; Jerem. 3: 1-10; Isa. 54: 4-5; Cant. Cf. also D. Buzy, *"L'allégorie matrimoniale de*

Jahvé et d'Israël et le Cantique des Cantiques," in *Vivre et Penser*, III, 77-90.

49. Cf. M. J. Lagrange, *Évangile selon saint Jean* (Paris, 1925), p. 61; O. Cullmann, *op. cit.*, p. 39; F. M. Braun, *op. cit.*, p. 69.

50. Lagrange, *loc. cit.*

51. Cullmann insists on the connection between miracle and sacrament to the point of making them equivalent: "It could be demonstrated that in a general way, the sacraments have for the Church the same signification that the miracles performed by Jesus had on his contemporaries" (*op. cit.*, p. 39). There is this difference, however, that the miracle has not of itself a spiritual efficacy comparable to that of the sacrament.

52. *Op. cit.*, p. 158. Gaechter even thinks that this comparison with the Pasch did not escape the mind of the Evangelist. Nevertheless, there is no positive proof of this.

Chapter IV

1. The chapter of the work cited, *Maria im Erdenleben*, which treats of this episode (pp. 201-226) is the revision of an article that appeared in 1923 in *Zeitschrist für katholische Theologie*, 47 (1923), 391-429.

2. F. M. Braun, *La Mère des fidèles*, p. 113.

3. *Ibid.*, pp. 109-113.

4. This is the opinion of Loisy, *Le quatrième Évangile* (Paris, 1921), p. 488. Already refuted by Lagrange, in *Évangile selon saint Jean* (Paris, 1925), p. 495, this was taken up again by Bultmann in his volume, *Das Evangelium des Johannes* (Göttingen, 1941), p. 521.

5. Braun, *op. cit.*, 124-218.

6. The expression $\varepsilon\iota\varsigma$ $\tau\alpha$ $\iota\delta\iota\alpha$ is found in two other places. "Voici que vient l'heure et elle est déjà venue, où vous vous disperserez chacun *chez soi*" (16, 32). "Il vint *chez lui*" (50, 11).

Notes

7. The two other prophecies (Isa. 7:14 and Mich. 5:2) relate to the birth of the Messiah and do not reveal any direct relation to the scene on Calvary.

8. Gaechter, *op. cit.*, pp. 205-212, 224-226; F. M. Braun, *op. cit.*, pp. 78-82.

9. Braun, *op. cit.*, pp. 82-87; cf. John 12: 31.

10. *Ibid.*, p. 93.

11. Confer particularly, H. Van den Bussche, *"Het wijnwonder te Cana (Jo. 2:1-2),"* in *Collationes Gandavenses,* 35 (1952), 218; J. Giblet, in *Collectanea Mechliniensia,* 38 (1953), 596, n. 2; A. M. Dubarle, *"Les fondements bibliques du titre marial de Nouvelle Ève,"* in *Melanges Lebreton,* I, *Recherches de Science Religieuse,* 39 (1951-1952), 64.

12. J. Giblet, *art. cit.*, p. 598, which characterizes the usual interpretation.

13. "Genesis I-III and St. John's Gospel," in *The Journal of Thelogical Studies,* XXI (1920), 210-218. Hoskyn draws a comparison regarding the communication of the vital breathing of the Holy Ghost to the disciples through the risen Christ and that of the Garden of Eden, the garden of the arrest and the garden of the resurrection.

14. In Saint John, the demon does not appear under the form of a serpent; Christ on the contrary compares himself to the brazen serpent (3:14ff.).

A NOTE ON THE TYPE
IN WHICH THIS BOOK IS SET

This book is set in Fairfield, a Linotype face, created by Rudolph Ruzicka, distinguished American artist and engraver. Introduced in 1940, Fairfield is almost strictly a book type with much charm and beauty. It is easy to read as one learns from extensive reading since it furnishes some degree of stimulation and pleasure to the eye. The fitting of each letter is practically perfect, which is a real tribute to its designer. This book was printed and composed by Lewis Printing Company of Richmond, Virginia, and bound by Moore and Company of Baltimore. The typography and design by Howard N. King.

CARMELITE MONASTERY
Beckley Hill
Barre, Vt., 05641

DATE BORROWED